# Writers and Politics
# in Nigeria

## James Booth

# AFRICANA PUBLISHING COMPANY

## NEW YORK

*A division of Holmes & Meier Publishers, Inc.*

*Acknowledgements*
The publishers would like to thank the following for permission to reproduce copyright material:

Rex Collings Ltd (UK and Commonwealth rights, *Season of Anomy*, by Wole Soyinka)
Mr W. Soyinka (US rights, *Season of Anomy*)
Andre Deutsch Ltd (UK and Commonwealth rights, *The Interpreters*, by Wole Soyinka)

First published in the United States of America 1981 by
Africana Publishing Company
A division of Holmes & Meier Publishers, Inc.
30 Irving Place, New York, N.Y. 10003

**Library of Congress Cataloging in Publication Data**

Booth, James, 1945-
    Writers and politics in Nigeria.

Bibliography: p.
1. Nigerian fiction (English)—History criticism. 2. Politics and literature—Nigeria. 3. Politics in literature. I. Title
PR9387.4.B66 1980 823'.009 80-17670
ISBN 0-8419-0650-5
ISBN 0-8419-0651-3 (pbk.)

Printed in Malta

# Contents

121608

# 1 Perspectives

## Writers and politics in Africa

Conceptual problems unknown in Europe and North America confront the political thinker and the imaginative writer in an independent African state. Society in the developed world presents a familiar spectrum of politics from right to left: fascism, conservatism, liberalism, christian and social democracy, marxism and marxism-leninism. It is mapped in terms of conflicting and evolving classes: the land-owning aristocracy, the bourgeoisie, petty bourgeoisie, proletariat and peasantry. Events and movements are easily placed within a developing historical context of competing ideologies based on socio-economic classes. The writer in the West can, if he wishes, take a confident ideological stance. T.S. Eliot roundly pronounces himself 'classicist in literature, royalist in politics, and anglo-catholic in religion'.[1] Jean-Paul Sartre directs the writer to pronounce on public affairs 'not from the point of view of an abstract morality, but in the perspectives of a precise goal which is the realization of a socialist democracy'. [2] Alternatively the Western writer may reject political commitment in favour of 'abstract morality' or pure aestheticism. In either case he asserts his individuality in terms of a rich store of categories and historical precedents shared with his readers.

The modern African cannot feel so certain of his political and ideological context. To some extent the political and aesthetic categories evolved in Europe must also apply in Africa. Human societies share some common characteristics everywhere. However, the African politician or writer in a newly independent state is understandably reluctant to accept without radical reassessment the system of ideas imposed by

5

the colonist. The first step of political emancipation having been achieved he is wary of re-enslaving himself by a kind of cultural neo-colonialism, to non-African concepts and ideals whose relevance to his situation is questionable. In some respects post-colonial Africa finds itself in a new situation, one quite unprecedented in the history of Europe. While open to the most modern influences in technology and ideas, most African states still have largely agricultural economies in which traditional cultural values retain their power. Class differentiation is at a very early stage. Will Africa then necessarily develop similar social and political structures to those of Europe? Are there perhaps new, purely African possibilities for combining the traditional with the modern? Some politicians and some writers think that there are. A complicating factor here is that Africa, unlike Europe, has to cope in its development with the prior existence of an immensely powerful developed world which has in the past dominated its political and cultural life and still attempts to do so in the present. For the writer this means that the publishing and distribution of African books has been largely in the hands of Western companies and, more radically, that many of the books themselves are written in European languages. In these circumstances the effort required to escape external pressures and achieve an independent identity is clearly great. For the politician the task is to mould a national identity within the arbitrary boundaries left by the colonist, and within a world-system dominated by the developed nations. For the writer it is to express an authentic African identity within the colonist's language and literary conventions.

One way in which the African may seek an identity is by returning imaginatively to the pre-colonial past. This is the recourse of a number of novelists who attempt a re-creation of traditional life as it was before the European intrusion, or as it persists, secluded from direct European influence. *L'Enfant Noir*[3](1954) by the Guinean, Camara Laye, was the first such work. Its tone is reminiscent of that of the European pastoral, but the social and religious customs which it describes are very different from those of Europe. It has however been criticised for sentimentalising its subject. Chinua Achebe for instance finds it 'a little too sweet'.[4] In Nigeria Achebe's own novels of traditional village life, *Things Fall Apart* (1958) and *Arrow of God* (1964) take a rather more complex approach, involving the reader's sympathies through a detailed evocation of an harmonious traditional culture before introducing the destructive and uncomprehending whites. Achebe sees this task of cultural retrieval as one of the primary duties of the African writer in the first years of independence.

> Here then is an adequate revolution for me to espouse—to help my society regain belief in itself and put away the complexes of the years of denigration and self-abasement.[5]

It is an act of political commitment to celebrate the African past after years of colonial distortion. Achebe is however, as his remark on Laye shows, aware of the pitfalls of such a commitment. The element of idyllic pastoral must not be allowed to degenerate into escapist oversimplification. And the artist must not compromise his integrity by resorting to propaganda. If the colonist could see little good in African traditions, it is equally a distortion to see no bad in them.

> The credibility of the world he is attempting to re-create will be called to question and he will defeat his own purpose if he is suspected of glossing over inconvenient facts. We cannot pretend that our past was one long, technicolour idyll.[6]

Perhaps the most interesting variant on such distortion is to be found in the strange symbolic novel, *Two Thousand Seasons* (1973) by the Ghanaian, Ayi Kwei Armah. Armah avoids the pitfall of overt glamorisation by describing his golden age only in retrospective glimpses, the main line of the narrative being concerned with the attacks of the 'predators' (Arabs) and 'destroyers' (whites) of the African 'way'. We learn from these scattered communal memories that 'Ours . . was the way of creation. From the cycle of regeneration we had not yet strayed on this exile road.'[7] An early age of violent patriarchy, we are told, gave way to the benign rule of women.

7

The time following—it is that we still call the fertile time—was creation's time. In its abundance generosity became our vice. We lost the quick suspiciousness of the deprived, gained unwisely generous reflexes, grew able to give without having to worry about receiving . . .[8]

The novel's obsessively violent accounts of the invaders who take advantage of this innocent generosity and pervert or destroy 'the way' reveal Armah's propagandist, not to say racist, intention.

We are not stunted in spirit, we are not Europeans, we are not Christians that we should invent fables a child would laugh at and harden our eyes to preach them daylight and deep night as truth. We are not so warped in soul, we are not Arabs, we are not Muslims to fabricate a desert god chanting madness in the wilderness, and call our creature creator. That is not our way.[9]

This novel seems to illustrate Armah's own critical remark, made in a different context.

Negative, anti-colonial feeling is relatively easy to come by. At any rate it does not demand any genius. The development of positive programmes and ideologies is a much more difficult proposition.[10]

The nearest we come in *Two Thousand Seasons* to a positive programme is in the story of a band of blacks who escape from a slave ship before it has left Africa, and devote themselves religiously to the systematic killing of whites. The element of wish-fulfilment fantasy is strong, and Wole Soyinka has praised the novel as a useful attempt to exorcise the feelings of helplessness induced by colonialism. It is, he says, 'a visionary reconstruction of the past for the purposes of social direction'.[11] The function of its grim catalogue of violence is thus a kathartic one; it serves as a psychological preparation for positive action. In itself however the novel is negative. Its positive idea, 'the way', remains hazy and ill-defined and the only 'social direction' it asserts is resistance to oppression.

Propagandist simplifications of a similar kind to those found in the novelists are made by those political thinkers who build upon the supposed pristine pre-European or non-European consciousness, whole ideologies of 'Africanness',

'the African Soul', or 'African socialism'. The classic illustration of such an attempt to erect an African ideology in
opposition to the simplifications of Europe is the Négritude
movement. And it is now generally recognized that in fact it
merely reproduced the European stereotype of the noble
savage: simple, spontaneous and intuitive. The importance of
Négritude lies not in any philosophical profundity, but in its
use of this stereotype as a moral and political weapon in the
struggle against white domination. The poetry of Négritude
extols the purity of the Negro soul, always in implied contrast
with corrupt, imperialistic Europe. It appeals to the white
man's better self in the terms of his own racial myths.

Mercy for our omniscient and naive conquerors!

Eia for grief at the udders of reincarnated tears
For those who explored nothing
For those who never mastered

Eia for joy
Eia for love [12]

These famous lines by Aimé Césaire the surrealist poem from
Martinique who first coined the term 'Négritude', imply
(reasonably enough, perhaps) that it is only by suppressing joy
and love that the cruder whites have achieved their dominance
over the more sensitive Negroes. Confronted with the scientific
and technological mastery of white civilisation Négritude fell
back on the most obvious 'opposite' qualities and labelled
them 'Negro'. In the words of Soyinka it 'extolled the
apparent'.[13] White culture is exact, analytical and intellectual
(ignoring for the argument's sake much of its music, painting
and poetry). Black culture must therefore be emotional,
intuitive, rhythmical. In the absurd dictum of the most
prominent exponent of Négritude, the President of Senegal,
Léopold Sédar Senghor: 'Emotion is completely Negro as
reason is Greek'.[14] Soyinka comments drily that Négritude
'accepted one of the most commonplace blasphemies of
racism, that the black man has nothing between his ears, and
proceeded to subvert the power of poetry to glorify this
fabricated justification of European cultural domination'.[15]

9

It is important to recognize the intimate association of Négritude with the French colonial policy of *assimilation*. It was in origin essentially a practical expedient in the resistance to imperialism. The term was taken up as a slogan in the 1930s by the elite of France's West Indian and African subjects who were studying in Paris as part of France's grand plan to make them into black Frenchmen—to assimilate them. It was not a fully worked-out system of ideas but an expression of cultural alienation by men who were being systematically stripped of their cultural identity. This is clear from Senghor's account.

> Paradoxically, it was the French who first forced us to seek its essence and who then shewed us where it lay when they enforced their policy of assimilation and thus deepened our despair. We set out on a fervent quest for the 'holy grail'—our collective soul.[16]

(It is a significant comment on *assimilation* that Senghor should choose a romantic legend from medieval Europe as an image for this quest for his African identity.) Senghor is quite explicit as to the racism of Négritude at this early stage.

> The revolt was purely negative. I confess it. The Negro students of whom I was one in the years 1930-4 were negativists. I confess we were racists. We were delirious in our négritude. No dialogue was then possible with Europe.[17]

Our analysis would suggest that Négritude was on the contrary, essentially part of a dialogue with Europe. Subsequent assertions of a black culture distinct from the white have been most intense in situations where blacks have felt themselves similarly threatened with domination or assimilation; in the West Indies for instance where there is no indigenous culture to oppose that of Europe, in the United States where blacks are a minority, and in South Africa where 'Black Consciousness' is a political weapon against oppression. It has been said that Négritude failed to 'catch on' to any large extent in the British African colonies because British policy with its 'Indirect Rule' left indigenous cultures in many respects to themselves. Although Nkrumah's 'African Personality' in Ghana was a version of Négritude, and various theories of a distinctively African socialism have been adopted by other political leaders,

10

Anglophone writers and intellectuals have rarely been enthusiastic about them. Chinua Achebe sums up the general feeling.

> You have all heard of the African Personality; of African democracy, of the African way to socialism, of négritude, and so on. They are all props we have fashioned at different times to help us get on our feet again. Once we are up we shan't need any of them any more. But for the moment it is in the nature of things that we may need to counter racism with what Jean-Paul Sartre has called an anti-racist racism, to announce not just that we are as good as the next man but that we are much better.[18]

Senghor however has continued to cling to Négritude. He now considers that the 'holy grail' of the Negro soul has been found and that henceforth Negro culture 'complements'[19] that of Europe. His own poetry reveals very clearly the ambiguities of such a claim. It shows an intensely romantic nostalgia for Africa, but an Africa strangely abstracted by French literary fashion into a mysterious symbolist evanescence. The poet's elegant and refined sensibility constantly evokes images of the glamorous, the precious, the dreamy and far away.

> Diamond patiently cut by a famous House
> Your smile sets me a riddle, subtler than those
> exchanged among the Confederate Princes. [20]

> Our cloth is white gold, the clouds are red gold our
> lofty seignorial standard. [21]

> [for khalam]
> And we shall be steeped my dear in the presence of
> Africa.
> Furniture from Guinea and Congo, heavy and polished,
> sombre and serene.
> On the walls, pure primordial masks distant and yet
> present.
> Stools of honour for hereditary guests, for the
> Princes of the High Lands. [22]

(Notice that the specific parts of Africa he mentions both happen to be French-speaking.) This is a 'primordial', mys-

11

terious Africa seen through the medium of a French 'decadent' poetic sensibility. It is astonishing how far away and elusive the 'Africa' of this African writer sounds: and not simply with the distance to be expected in the poetry of an exile far from home (many of his poems were written in France) but with the intrinsic, aesthetic, literary distance so beloved of the symbolist imagination. It is difficult to avoid the conclusion that Senghor has in fact been successfully assimilated. Emancipation on the political level seems to have left colonisation on the cultural level unaffected. Leaving aside the explicit ethnic allusions, few readers could guess that the writer of this poetry was not a conservative French bourgeois modernist, with his elusive symbolist manner and his reverential awe before the ultra-*chic* of diamonds cut by famous houses and the gorgeous aristocratic medieval past. It is not surprising that Senghor should have translated T.S. Eliot's most subtle work, *Four Quartets*, into French.

A writer who is well aware of the dangers of the self-consciously racial approach to the search for an African identity is Wole Soyinka from whose critique of Négritude I have already quoted. Soyinka nevertheless still insists on the existence of a distinctively African world-view. But although his attempts to define it contain much that is stimulating and provocative, they succeed ultimately little better than Senghor's. He makes a highly metaphysical distinction between Africa and Europe which owes something to the Dionysiac/Apollonian distinction in Nietzsche's *The Birth of Tragedy*, a strong early influence on his aesthetic thought. The tendency to think dialectically in opposing categories is, he feels, European. Europe is Manichean whereas Africa is radically un-Manichean. It is alien, he says, to '*the* African world-view' [my italics] to conceive 'that there are watertight categories of the creative spirit, that creativity is not one smooth-flowing source of human regeneration'.[23] Many a nineteenth-century English Romantic uses virtually the same words to define his particular *European* world-view. The rather vapid rhetoric of the last phrase here makes one wonder how genuinely felt this idea is and even, indeed, whether, despite all his disclaimers, Soyinka is not re-introducing, in less obvious guise, the idea of the 'intuitive' Negro which he mocks in the Négritudinists. His concluding passage on this topic is one of masterly wit, but it is very indirect and very 'clever'. He portrays Descartes himself, confident in his philosophical categories, 'engaged in the mission of piercing the jungle of the black pre-logical mentality with his intellectual canoe'. Confronted by 'our mythical brother innocent' in his 'virginal village' he intones 'I think, therefore I am'. According to Soyinka the African would not respond like the Négritudinists *within* the Cartesian categories, with 'I feel, therefore I am', but would

> reduce our white explorer to syntactical proportions by responding: 'You think, therefore you are a thinker. You are one-who-thinks, white-creature-in-pith-helmet-in-African-jungle-who-thinks and, finally, white-man-who-has-problems-believing-in-his-own-existence.' And I cannot believe that he would arrive at that observation solely by intuition.[24]

This is brilliant and thought-provoking precisely because of its idiosyncracy. Its casual, anecdotal form makes no pretension to formulate or define in the sober, direct way of the ideologist. Perhaps in the end this sort of thing is the most effective achievement to be expected from this line of approach to the African identity through the search for the pristine African consciousness. It may indeed be possible to make systematic distinctions between the Celtic, Negro, Teutonic, Latin or Semitic world-views; or between Asian, American, African and European world-views. And in the nineteenth and early twentieth centuries, the great age of metaphysics (and also of imperialism) it was fashionable to do so. But history shows the dangers of such an approach, and the diversity of culture and individuality within such huge sections of humankind makes it a very provisional and subjective exercise. Moreover the production of culture itself, in the form of literature, art, music, philosophy and science must always be immeasurably more effective than any theorising, in establishing cultural identity.

13

Soyinka himself illustrates a quite different approach to this problem when he focuses on the precise political and social implications of Négritude. The philosophical and aesthetic inadequacy of Négritude can be seen as the manifestation of a more tangible political inadequacy. It is significant that several of the strongest exponents of the philosophy of 'the African Soul' are or were political leaders, Sékou Touré of Guinea for instance, Nkrumah of Ghana and of course Senghor of Senegal. To Soyinka, and to the Ghanaian, Ayi Kewi Armah, the lesson is clear. Such philosophies, however innocent their origins, have become, with independence, a political device used by the nation's elite to divert attention from their failure to introduce any radical changes in the colonial structure. The black rulers have simply stepped into the place of their white predecessors. Soyinka mocks Jean-Paul Sartre's idea that the emotional affirmation of Negroness can still be a revolutionary force once its original anti-colonial purpose has been served.

> As for the pipe-dream of Sartre that it would pass through stages of development and merge itself within the context of the proletarian fight, one would have thought that it was obvious enough that Négritude was the property of a bourgeois-intellectual elite, and that there was therefore far greater likelihood that it would become little more than a diversionary weapon in the eventual emergence of a national revolutionary struggle wherever the flag-bearers of Négritude represent the power-holding elite.[25]

According to Armah the leadership of independent Africa is engaged in a confidence trick played on its own people, an attempt to pretend that 'a manifestly *evolutionary* situation' is *'revolutionary'*.[26] Senghor's Négritude and Nkrumah's 'African Personality' are to Armah mere mystifications, 'sloganeering gimmicks' designed to persuade the people that the substitution of black oppressors for white is real liberation. The grandiose verbiage of Nkrumah seems to support Armah's point.

> I believe strongly and sincerely that with the deep-rooted wisdom and dignity, the innate respect for human lives, the intense humanity

14

that is our heritage, the African race, united under one federal government, will emerge not as just another world bloc to flaunt its wealth and strength, but as a Great Power whose greatness is indestructible because it is built not on fear, envy and suspicion, nor won at the expense of others, but founded on hope, trust, friendship and directed to the good of all mankind.[27]

Sincere or not, these words can scarcely be said to address themselves to the realities of post-independence Africa.

The great analyst of neo-colonialism, Frantz Fanon, criticises the concept of a distinct black culture more succinctly.

To believe that it is possible to create a black culture is to forget that niggers are disappearing. [28]

In other words the very consciousness of a distinct, oppressed black ('nigger') identity needing expression, is the product of social and political forces which are retreating with the gradual political awakening of black Africa. For Fanon identity is not to be sought in inherent racial qualities, but in socio-economic forces. The road forward to a new African role in the world is therefore not through racial introspection, but through political change, through revolution. One of the most valuable contributions of Fanon to the search for an African identity is his analysis of colonial and post-colonial society in terms of class-formation. The key element in such societies in his view is the growth and accession to power of what he calls an 'under-developed bourgeoisie'. It is this class which defends its hegemony by promoting, and even believing itself, obscurantist doctrines of racial liberation, when it is its own existence which prevents the true *human* liberation of the people. It is to this dominant class that both politicians and writers belong.

The bourgeoisie of colonial or ex-colonial countries differs radically, as Fanon's phrase indicates, from its European counterparts. In Europe the bourgeoisie arose as the result of historical forces organic to society, as a dynamic enterprising class, generating wealth by entrepreneurial skills and the creation and exploitation of capital. In the colonial world the bourgeoisie is not in any significant sense a creator of

15

capital, but the artificial creation of a capitalist system whose centre is in Europe (and latterly in the United States). The colonialist and the neo-colonialist are, naturally enough, concerned with the economic and political development of the colony or ex-colony only to the extent that it serves their own economic interests. This results in what has been called 'the development of underdevelopment'.[29] The economy of the 'developing' country is not permitted by its developed trading partners to generate its own momentum, or goals appropriate to the needs of its people as a whole. Instead it is cajoled or coerced by trade agreements and development projects into functioning as a supplier of raw material and a purchaser of high technology and surplus manufactures. Within this system members of the indigenous bourgeoisie perform the essential function of agents or middle-men to foreign interests, for which they are rewarded with wealth and with political (and sometimes military) support. The bourgeoisie is essentially a client.

> The national bourgeoisie of under-developed countries is not engaged in production, nor in invention, nor building, nor labour; it is completely canalised into activities of the intermediary type. Its innermost vocation seems to be to keep in the running and to be part of the racket. [30]

Independence brings no radical change in this unhappy state of dependence. 'The neocolonial lesson', as Basil Davidson remarks, is 'that economic hegemony need have no quarrel with the trappings of political self rule'.[31] The bourgeoisie, entrenched by the time of independence in its political domination of the 'new' nation, continues as before to function as commissioned middle-man. The structure remains unaltered.

One of the most prominent characteristics of this new under-developed bourgeois class, only a generation or less away from subsistence, is its ingenuous passion for the luxurious accessories of life as lived in the developed world. This passion is fostered by the West where the newly independent nations are seen increasingly as a market for manufactured goods. One of the most distressing aspects of the post-colonial world is the hectic scramble by the bourgeoisie for the luxury goods offered by the West, which stifles any attempt to develop a sound economic base on which to build national prosperity and an authentic political and cultural identity. The resources of the nation, instead of being devoted to the essentials of civilised life such as social services and public amenities, go largely to feed the private whims of the elite. As Fanon remarks:

> large sums are spent on display: on cars, country houses, and on all those things which have been justly described by economists as characterizing an under-developed bourgeoisie.[32]

The title of a novel by the Nigerian, Nkem Nwankwo, puts it in a nutshell: *My Mercedes is Bigger than Yours*. As we shall see, this betrayal of the new nation by the bourgeoisie is a central theme in Nigerian literature.

There have been many attempts to deny the validity of this analysis of modern African society in terms of socio-economic classes. Significantly in view of what has already been said such attempts often emanate from established political leaders. Several of the exponents of 'African socialism' argue that a quite new form of social organization is in the process of evolving in Africa, based on the extended family of traditional rural life, and bypassing the class struggle. Madeira Keita, former Minister of the Interior of Mali, takes this view.

> Naturally, we cannot claim that black African society is a classless society. But we do say that the differentiation between classes in Africa does not imply a diversification of interests, nor above all a clash of interests.[33]

Julius Nyerere of Tanzania argues similarly:

> The true African socialist does not look on one class of man as his brethren and another as his natural enemies. He does not form an alliance with the 'brethren' for the extermination of the 'non-brethren'. He rather regards *all* men as his brethren—as members of his ever extending family.[34]

17

This is clearly an attractive doctrine to rulers of one-party states, whether they make any serious attempt to put it into practice or not.

More practical and empirical is the analysis of Nigerian society by the American sociologist, Margaret Peil. She argues that traditional values have survived into the modern state with only 'minor modifications'.[35] Traditionally the Nigerian solves his or her social problems not through impersonal institutions of the modern kind, but through an elaborate system of personal contacts, based on patronage, the giving of inducements and family and regional ties.

It is quite clear that Nigerian society is built on, and functions through, personal relationships. Access to government is indirectly obtained through voting, but really important access depends on contacts... [36]

In Peil's view a true assessment of this peculiarly Nigerian blend of old and new demands a radical rethinking of European ideas, both of morality and of social organisation. The bribery, nepotism and ethnic favouritism which abound in Nigeria, for instance, cannot in her view be condemned out of hand as 'corruption'. They should be viewed more positively, as long-established patterns of behaviour.

Corruption cannot be rooted out because many forms of it are widely acceptable to the general public, conforming to their norms of proper behaviour by those who attain positions of leadership... [37]

Peil's analysis helps to account for the peculiar brazenness and apparent cynicism of Nigerian corruption as portrayed in the novels of Aluko, Achebe and Soyinka. However, the novelists do not fully share Peil's moral detachment. They may understand that the causes of such corruption lie deep in traditional habits, but they still condemn its perpetrators, however regretfully.

Despite the usefulness of her analyses of the particular mechanisms of Nigerian society, Peil's view that economic class-formation is not taking place in Nigeria cannot be accepted. She argues that the 'Marxist' interpretation (by which she means simply one in terms of classes) is not applicable to Nigeria, since economic interest is traditionally not the basis of a citizen's social identity or political allegiance. Geo-ethnic loyalties and all kinds of personal connections, from bribery to family ties, serve to confound the European distinctions.

> Since urban/rural and occupational classifications are seldom productive of attitude differences, parties based on these interests (i.e. Marxist parties) seem unlikely to attract many members.[38]

This is an accurate account of the political situation as it is at present, but Peil's implication that this is an essential and permanent departure from the European pattern is questionable.

> ... in spite of the confident predictions of Marxist observers, a class system has not yet developed in Nigeria. [39]

The key word here is, of course 'yet'. How long does Margaret Peil consider necessary for the development of class identity and class-consciousness? Nigeria, it must be remembered, became independent a mere twenty years ago. The longer historical perspective of Basil Davidson seems a more sound one. In his view the same basic economic forces are at work in Africa as have been at work in Europe, despite the many important differences.

> An interesting parallel has been drawn between the corruptions and coercions of eighteenth-century England and twentieth-century Nigeria, and it could certainly be extended, both in time and place. Yet the parallel arises not from any particular venality of the peoples in question, even of the English, but from parallel efforts at building capitalist systems. The one, like the other, took the only possible means of making middle classes grow and prosper to the point at which they can exercise hegemony: that is, by the despoilment of others in the state; while not forgetting, of course, that in due time the poachers will turn gamekeepers, and wax in wrath at any least attack upon the sacred rights of property.[40]

It is difficult not to acknowledge the force of this parallel with Europe. And it is surely undeniable that classes *do*

19

already exist in Nigeria and elsewhere in Africa. Naturally the bourgeoisie is well ahead in its class solidarity, while the members of proletariat (such as it is) and peasantry have yet to evolve sufficient consciousness of shared interest to defend themselves, although resentment at the ostentatious wealth of the rich can already be very strong, regardless of ethnic or other loyalties. In a country which possesses its full complement of ostentatious millionaires, which has an acute problem of urban destitution, no system of social security, and holds frequent public executions of armed robbers, it is surely naive to speak of the sufficiency of traditional loyalties as an answer to people's political needs. Certainly the novelists would seem to incline towards Fanon's and Davidson's view rather than Peil's. Achebe's Chief Nanga is an excellent illustration of the destructiveness of the new bourgeois class. And in *Season of Anomy* (1973) Soyinka identifies the true enemy, through all the confusions of ethnic bigotry behind which it hides itself, as an economic interest group—the Cartel. It may be that traditional attitudes complicate the socio-economic picture at this early stage, and that resentment at social injustice may only too easily be directed into atavistic channels. But it is the woolliest liberalism to imagine that the personal patronage and string-pulling of traditional Nigerian life can permanently modify economic realities to the point of rendering society 'classless'.

The natural function of the African writer then will be similar to that of the European writer in the eighteenth and nineteenth centuries. He acts as both the consciousness and the conscience of the culturally dominant class to which he, inevitably, belongs. In writers like Fielding and Dickens we find on the one hand, a celebration of the bourgeois virtues and, on the other, satire on the bourgeois vices. The greatest writers, such as Sterne or George Eliot, begin even to perceive the limitations of the bourgeois virtues. In Africa, however, the peculiarly hollow and flimsy nature of the new bourgeoisie makes the writer's role in relation to it more uncomfortable than it was in Europe. The European writer could at least usually identify himself with the 'better self' of his class, its more permanent and worthwhile ideals. And it was, after all, a creative and dynamic class at the ideological growing point of his society. In Africa the writer is likely to feel quite alienated from the under-developed bourgeoisie, and so radically unsure of his artistic role. Moreover the general lack of literacy and education (and the fact that he is almost certainly writing in a European language) cut him off from the wider populace, and isolate him within this corrupt and materialistic elite. His books themselves are (at least in the early years) part of a commercial market largely external to his own country. Many of his readers, (in some cases the majority of them), come from the developed world. Worse still, the very forms and styles of his literary art may easily seem a spiritual parallel to the foreign luxury goods in which the members of the elite indulge themselves. Has Soyinka for instance, with his modernist techniques, obscure symbolism and arcane vocabulary, deserted the real interests of his new nation for the *cultural* luxury goods of the West? Ayi Kwei Armah presents a despairing version of this question in the narrator of his novel *Why Are We So Blest?* (1972) who detests himself for describing, in the eloquent literary techniques of European narrative art, the spiritual destruction of the black protagonist of the novel by Europe. He accuses himself of being no better than the more obvious middle-men employed by the developed world to keep his people enslaved. The very act of writing may thus seem a betrayal, aligning the writer firmly with the developed world. The problem of language will be examined more fully in the next chapter, but enough has been said to show the formidable problems facing the African writer in his attempt to find a constructive role for his art within his society.

## Nigeria: federation and national culture

So far we have been concerned with the problems of neo-colonial dependence and cultural confusion faced by all independent black African states. Each country however

21

presents a different version of these problems, modified by its own unique history, geography and demography. Indeed it may often seem to the despairing observer that all attempts, by politician or writer, to confront the essential problems of post-colonial society, are doomed to be thwarted by the messy accidents of particular times and places: ethnic jealousies, the arbitrary national boundaries left by colonialism, even purely personal rivalries between members of tiny governing elites. In the case of Nigeria all such particular problems seem to focus on its very status as a 'nation', a role for which it seems less fitted than most other African states. Its constitution is, uniquely in Africa, a federal one. Since independence in 1960 both the nature and the number of the units making up the federation have changed several times. First there were three 'regions', later increased to four, then (briefly) twenty-one 'provinces', then twelve 'states', and now there are nineteen states. The right balance of power between central federal authority and local administration has proved extremely difficult to find.

The immediate and urgent priority for any newly-formed nation is the establishment of a sense of national identity and of national unity. In the early years most African ex-colonies made at least some show of success, however dubious, in this difficult task. Zambia, Tanzania, Kenya, Ghana and Senegal all presented, in the period immediately following independence, a strong appearance of unity under a charismatic leader, a 'father of the nation', who actively promoted a 'national' ideology: Zambian (Christian) humanism, African socialism, the African Personality or Négritude. In Nigeria such a show of unified national consciousness (however flimsy) was scarcely possible. The various African socialisms for instance, with their stress on the (ever-extending) family, though most useful in nations such as Tanzania with few ethnic tensions, would be more likely to foster division in a nation so ethnically diverse as Nigeria. The obvious candidate in Nigeria for national leadership of the Nyerere-Kenyatta kind, Nnamdi Azikiwe, could clearly never achieve this status, because as an Easterner his motives were suspect in the eyes of Westerners and Northerners. Such suspicions as these have been a central element in Nigerian politics. It can be argued that the regional diversity of Nigeria confers certain advantages. Chief Obafemi Awolowo, former premier of the Western Region, felt that 'the heterogeneous character of the peoples of Nigeria is in itself a potential check on the emergence of a totalitarian form of government'.[41] And this argument possesses a certain force. It is difficult to imagine a Bokassa or an Amin ever gaining control in a nation with so many large and powerful minorities. Nevertheless this ethnic and cultural diversity does also constitute the greatest barrier to national unity and thus to the formation of a national culture from which a truly 'Nigerian' literature may arise.

The problem is inherent in the very concept of 'Nigeria', that 'arbitrary block'[42] carved out of Africa by the British, and including within its borders peoples with cultures, histories and languages as different from each other as those of Britain and China. Nigeria came into existence during the 'Scramble for Africa' which followed the Berlin Conference of the imperial powers (1884-5). At first the North and South of the colonial 'Protectorate' remained quite separate. And, as Ruth First remarks, when the two territories were brought nominally under one administration in 1914, 'the only bond of political unity was the person of Lugard, the governor-general'.[43] Indeed, it was not until the setting up of the Legislative Assembly in 1946 that Northerners and Southerners actually sat together on any Nigerian consultative or governing body. Political power in the North, where communications are relatively good, has always tended to be centralised. As Michael Crowder remarks: 'In the open savannah of the north, the organization of large political units was much easier than in the dense forests of the south.'[44] In the nineteenth century this power fell to the Islamic Fulani through a *jihad* or war of conversion, which imposed the feudal and aristocratic system known as the Hausa-Fulani emirates. A vivid and highly coloured impression of life in the North during the colonial period can be gained from the early novels of the Anglo-Irish writer Joyce Cary, who was in the Nigerian Political Service

23

from 1913 until 1919. The action of his first published novel, *Aissa Saved* (1932), centres on the attempts of Bradgate, a harassed District Officer to restrain the aggressive fervour of a group of Christian converts who wage a holy war on their pagan neighbours, abetted by a naive British missionary couple. Bradgate's Moslem protegé, Ali, seems to be the best hope for the future with his enthusiasm for the sound British virtues of duty, uprightness and impartiality. But he is tortured to death by the Christians when he attempts to stand in their way. The Moslem rulers are portrayed as effete, crafty and corrupt. The climax of the novel is one of bloodshed and chaos, as the Christians resort to human sacrifice and meet the pagans in pitched battle. As a conscientious administrator Cary endorses in this novel the official government policy in the North at that time: disapproval of disruptive missionary activity and co-operation with the Moslem emirs, even while recognizing their corruption. It is only such a policy, he implies, that can avert the kind of anarchy and violence which he portrays in the novel. Useful though it was however in preserving order under colonialism, this policy has had far-reaching consequences for modern Nigeria, by ensuring the educational and social backwardness of the North in comparison with the South. The effect of such attitudes on the part of the colonial administration was to isolate the North from many of the progressive influences which were transforming the South, and to preserve in power an autocratic and archaic ruling class.

In the South Christian missionary activity, and the Western education that went with it, met with great success, especially in the East. Thus a primary source of potential division in Nigeria has been an antagonism between North and South; the South more advanced, better educated, and Christian or traditional in religion, the North backward and Islamic. At independence the constitution bequeathed by Britain stipulated that representation in parliament should be on the basis of population. The North proving far more populous than the South (although the census was fiercely questioned) thus retained a built-in and indefinite political control of the

Federation, a fact much resented in the South. Conversely the North has always suspected that the more dynamic, Westernised Southerners will seek to dominate it politically. National unity under these circumstances can only be a matter of compromises and balances of power. During the period of civilian rule which followed independence (1960-6) government depended on coalitions between the North and one or other of the main ethnic groups of the South, the Ibos of the East or the Yorubas of the West. The idea of a 'national culture' in such a situation must seem a mere pipe-dream.

During the colonial period it never proved possible to govern the country effectively as a unit: each region presented its own particular problems. Lord Lugard's policy of 'Indirect Rule' (adopted for reasons of economy) worked best in the North where a well-established political structure already existed. The emirs acted as tax-gatherers and agents for the colonial power in return for its support and a large degree of internal autonomy. In the West the system of 'warrant chiefs', chosen from among the local traditional rulers, worked reasonably well since it could rely on an existing aristocracy of 'obas' or chiefs, though one much less rigid and stable than that in the North. The strong and widespread Yoruba traditional religion resisted (and resists) Christianity more effectively than the more localised religions of the East, but it did not present any serious political threat to the colonial authorities. In the East however the traditional social organisation was quite different, as one can see from the historical novels of Ibo village life by Chinua Achebe. In *Things Fall Apart* and *Arrow of God*, we are introduced to a society where consensus seems as important as authority; a kind of communalist democracy tempered by patriarchy, where law and custom are a function of the whole community rather than an imposition from above. Such a politically decentralised society was quite unprepared for the imposition of 'chiefs' by the central colonial authority. The action of *Arrow of God* concerns this moment in Nigerian history. The authorities choose a local priest of the god Ulu, who being the most respected man in the community is considered the most

25

suitable candidate for the post of Warrant Chief. The result is a head-on clash between different concepts of society. The priest, Ezeulu, flatly refuses to accept personal temporal power of a kind disapproved of by his community. Indeed he considers the offer an insult to his true spiritual role:

'Tell the white man that Ezeulu will not be anybody's chief, except Ulu.[45]

The confrontation brings disaster on the village. Ezeulu, imprisoned for his 'insolence', isolates himself within his pride and refuses when released to change the rate at which he eats the sacred yams. Since harvest cannot begin until these yams are consumed the livelihood of the people is threatened and they begin to question the wisdom of their priest. The colonialist's attempt to bring an orderly administration to this previously harmonious society thus causes chaos and demoralisation. A different, but common, result of the imposition of warrant chiefs was the exacerbation of local rivalries. The representatives of hitherto well-balanced factions would vie for the favour of the whites, with the unprecedented power it now conferred. Or, in the absence of traditional chiefs, unscrupulous and ruthless individuals would step into the gap. Better educated men from the coast would use their greater access to the whites to tyrannise over those further inland. And eventually the intense bitterness and resentment caused by such disruption of traditional habits and values forced the abandonment of this Indirect Rule policy in the Eastern Region. After the Aba riot of 1929 the Warrant Chiefs were withdrawn and direct rule re-instituted.

During the colonial period then the Ibos of the East, the Yorubas of the West and the Hausas of the North constituted quite separate social and political entities. This fact was recognised in the pre-Independence Nigerian constitutions. The Richards Constitution introduced in 1946 divided Nigeria into three 'Regions' each with a separate 'Deliberative Assembly'. Above these was a unitary 'Legislative Council'. When this system was replaced in 1954 by the Macpherson Constitution, agitation in the Western Region for greater autonomy and devolution of power was directed as much against central control *as such*, as against the colonial regime, while the fears of the Northern rulers that early Independence would surrender domination to the South made them equally anxious for as much regional devolution as possible. After Independence the problems persist. Indeed they are potentially more intense now that the centre, the federal authority, is no longer controlled by the alien colonialist, but by fellow-Nigerians with their own (real or suspected) ethnic and regional biases. The political turmoil of Nigeria during the 1960s was mainly caused by the fears within each Region that one or both of its rivals would take control of the centre and use the central power to limit its freedom.

The situation is further complicated by the existence beside these three large ethnic groups of the minorities—sometimes very large and influential minorities. These are chiefly concentrated in three areas: the Mid-West, inhabited by Urhobos and Itsekiris, traditionally dominated by the Yorubas; the Delta region, inhabited by Ijaws, Ibibios and others, traditionally dominated by the Ibos; and finally the Middle Belt, inhabited by Tivs, Kanuris and others, often non-Moslems, but dominated by the Moslems of the Hausa-Fulani North. In one respect these minorities are a great unifying force within the nation since they tend to favour a strong central government which will protect them from their more powerful neighbours. The existence of the minorities, however, constantly threatens to upset the balance of power between the majorities. In the period preceding Independence the East gave a great deal of support to the idea of a fourth Region to be created in the Mid-West, since this would deprive their Western rivals of territory and influence. In response the West supported the Delta minorities in their desire for separate status in the Federation in a COR (Calabar, Ogoja and Rivers) state, to be carved out of the East. And both Southern Regions naturally supported the setting up of a new Middle Belt Region which would weaken the North. The alarming instability of such a complex power balance with its potential for endless new coalitions and shifts of

27

allegiance, is obvious. In the period prior to Independence all these issues came to the surface as majorities and minorities manoeuvred for advantage. And Independence solved none of these radical constitutional problems. Indeed Chief Awolowo argued in his autobiography, published in the year of Independence (1960) that Britain's failure to act upon the findings of its Minorities Commission and create all three proposed new Regions at a stroke, condemned Nigeria to chronic instability. [46]

One inevitable result of the regional diversity of Nigeria has been that literature in English has developed at different rates in different areas. Any 'Nigerian' literature—any literature intended to have more than regional significance—must, for reasons discussed at greater length in the next chapter, be written in English (at least for the time being). Not surprisingly therefore, in view of the degree of early missionary penetration and the level of educational development, all the writers of national significance to have emerged so far have been Southerners: Yorubas, Ibos or members of the Southern minorities. Moreover within the South itself cultural diversity is inevitably reflected in the literature which has appeared. There are of course some universal themes. The rejection of colonial distortions for instance is a theme which will appeal to all citizens of newly independent nations, whatever their local preoccupations. Achebe explores this theme through what he knows at first hand, which is specifically Ibo, but the wider application is nevertheless perfectly clear. This is not however the case to the same degree with the school of writers who followed Achebe in the 1960s in creating heart-warming pictures of Ibo village life. Much of their work lacks Achebe's sense of wider issues and they thus seem provincial. These novelists: Nkem Nwankwo, Flora Nwapa, and John Munonye (Elechi Amadi, an Ikwerre from the adjacent Delta region, could be added) could be said to constitute an 'Ibo domestic school' of writing. Their characteristic gentle humour and warm sense of communal solidarity seem peculiar to their region. The West too has its characteristic literary forms and styles. Drama rather than the novel seems a natural preference

28

for several Yoruba writers, often with a ritualistic element derived from traditional religious festivals. Some of the plays of Soyinka, and those of Ola Rotimi and Duro Ladipo form a clear group of this kind. (John Pepper Clark, an Ijaw from the Delta region aligns himself in his plays with this Western group.) Again there is a distinction to be made between the writer who achieves a more universal level through his Yoruba material, as does Soyinka, and one whose appeal is primarily local, such as Rotimi. In itself there can be nothing wrong with cultural diversity. Any national literature is bound to have its roots in local and provincial particularities: witness Burns, Hardy and Lawrence in Britain. In Nigeria however, such distinct regional schools of writing uncomfortably emphasize the lack of the kind of cultural community which, despite diversity, does exist in Britain. More concretely they throw into prominence the lack of any comparable literature in English from the North. An observer seeking hard evidence of the existence of a 'Nigerian' culture must conclude that there is as yet no such thing: only Ibo culture, Yoruba culture, Hausa culture, etc.

The political upheavals of 1966-7 demonstrate in all its complexity the interaction between the national problems of post-colonial dependence and corruption, and the specific local problems of tribalism and disunity. The leader of the *coup* of January 1966, the idealistic and puritanical Major Nzeogwu seems to have been motivated entirely by 'Nigerian' motives. He was disgusted at the excesses of the ruling elite *as a class*, irrespective of ethnic considerations. He was a Nigerian first and an Ibo second. (As a Mid-West Ibo he belonged to a group which sometimes dissociates itself from the Ibos of the heartland.) His second name, Kaduna, refers to his place of birth in the North. He had lived much of his life in the North, spoke Hausa fluently and had many Hausa friends. His plan was to strike simultaneously at both regionalism and corruption by assassinating the rulers of all three major Regions. It is clear from the broadcast which he made on Radio Kaduna the day after the assassinations that he saw his actions entirely in the 'Nigerian' context.

Our enemies are the political profiteers, the swindlers, the men in the high and low places that seek bribes and demand ten per cent; those that seek to keep the country divided permanently so that they can remain in office as Ministers and VIPs of waste; the tribalists, the nepotists; those that made the country look big-for-nothing before the international circles; those that have corrupted our society and put the Nigerian political calendar back by their words and deeds . . . We promise that you will no more be ashamed to say that you are a Nigerian.[47]

It was by a characteristically tragic irony that the *coup* led by Nzeogwu resulted in the worst outbreak of violent 'tribalism' in recent Nigerian history. By accident and by the incompetence of his co-conspirators the task of assassination was thoroughly carried through only in the North, where Nzeogwu himself was in command. In the East the whole affair was botched: and in the West, although the Yoruba chauvinist and beneficiary of the shamelessly rigged 1965 election, Samuel Akintola, was killed, a crucial candidate for assassination, the Ibo, Major-General Aguyi-Ironsi, escaped. The result was that all the internal divisions of Nigeria were suddenly luridly highlighted in the eyes of the Northerners by what looked suspiciously like an Ibo-dominated plot aimed at taking control of the Federal government. This interpretation seemed confirmed when Ironsi persuaded his fellow-Ibo, Nzeogwu, to surrender power to him, and then in the following May proclaimed a new constitution abolishing the powerful Regions and setting up twenty-one 'Provinces' which would clearly be easily dominated by the (Ibo-controlled) centre. In the abstract such a measure might seem an excellent method of undercutting regional rivalries. Indeed a similar system has now been adopted. But at this time of heightened suspicion it could only arouse antagonism.

At the same time Ironsi threw open all civil service posts throughout the nation to unrestricted competition on merit, a move which would clearly have flooded the civil service with dynamic and well-educated Southerners. To the cry 'Araba', ('let us part') massacres of Ibos began in the North, Ironsi was assassinated and all the 'Nigerian' aims of the coup were forgotten in ethnic conflict. The committed 'Nigerian', Nzeogwu, compelled by events to participate in the 'Biafran' secession, became an embittered man. Indeed a rumour has circulated that his death in action fighting for Biafra in 1969 was in fact due to a conspiracy on his own side caused by his continued open criticism of the secession.

Nzeogwu's failure and disappointment can be seen to follow the same pattern as that of all Nigerian intellectuals during the 1960s, as the crude simplifications of tribal chauvinism shattered their ideal of a new unified and independent Nigerian nation. As one would expect, the early writers, educated abroad away from local rivalries, and acutely aware of the world context, show an intense nationalistic idealism over Nigeria. The cosmopolitan Easterners are particularly enthusiastic. Chinua Achebe gently satirises his own youthful idealism in the naive poem 'Nigeria' which the young protagonist of *No Longer At Ease* (1960) writes in London (in 1955).

> God bless our noble countrymen
> And women everywhere.
> Teach them to walk in unity
> To build our nation dear;
> Forgetting region, tribe or speech,
> But caring always each for each. [48]

*Beautiful Feathers* (1963) by the Northern-born Ibo, Cyprian Ekwensi, has an even wider, international perspective. The action concerns the leader of the Nigerian 'Movement for African and Malagasy Solidarity', who is an ardent pan-Africanist. Ekwensi dedicated the novel 'To Léopold Sédar Senghor of Négritude Fame and Alhaji Sir Abubakar Tafawa Balewa, Patron, Society of Nigerian Authors'[49] (and also of course a Northerner, a Moslem and Prime Minister of the Federation). To Nigerians with such wide perspectives as these the events of the summer of 1966 must have seemed a ghastly irrelevance to the essential problems of the new nation. But as massacres of Ibos increased and the exodus to the East from North and West began to create a *de facto*

31

secession events forced Eastern intellectuals to an abandonment of 'Nigeria' and support for the new 'Biafra'. A separate Ibo nation seemed at the time to offer the only hope for the future. This was a painful and difficult decision, made only when no other option seemed open, as can be seen from the letter by an unnamed Ibo quoted by Sunday Anozie, in which the decision of the poet Christopher Okigbo to volunteer for service in the Biafran army is discussed.

> After all it was a great shock, as you will yourself have experienced, in a short time to have to change political allegiance under the grim strains of the massacres and to feel that there was no hope or trust in the country that you had believed in all your life and that the only course was to create a new nation. [50]

It is difficult to see what other view the Ibo intellectual could have taken at this time. The writers played their part in the war effort. In 1969 Achebe toured the United States with his fellow-Biafrans, Cyprian Ekwensi and the Ijaw poet, Gabriel Okara, in an attempt to gain support for Biafra. Okigbo was killed in action in August 1967.

Among intellectuals in the Western Region in the early 1960s a similar 'Nigerian' idealism existed. No-one's contempt for prejudice and provincialism could be more robust than that of T.M. Aluko in his early novels, while Wole Soyinka goes so far as to record his wholehearted approval of the January *coup* and its aims.

> I could not, when the nature of the 15th January was finally digested, deny the rush of euphoria. I did and still wish that the revolt in the West had achieved victory as a people's uprising. Given a few more weeks this would have been realized. [51]

Generally speaking however, the secession was not so great a trauma in the West as in the East, where the population felt that its very life was being threatened. Soyinka nevertheless refused to keep quiet and wait for the war to end, and attempted practical action. At the outbreak of the massacres he travelled to the North in an attempt to create a united front against violence among all intellectuals. The disappointments he met with are harrowingly described in *The Man*

*Died* (1972).[52] He felt that the only answer lay with a 'Third Force' led by Victor Banjo, one of the original *coup*-plotters, a Yoruba ostensibly with the Biafran side. He began to advocate a UN ban on arms sales to either side in the conflict. Naturally enough his actions were interpreted by the Federal authorities as sedition and he was imprisoned for twenty-six months (1969-71). Soyinka's position was that the whole war was taking place on a false ground, it was an irrelevance to the nation's problems, and its outcome would be to embattle its rulers behind a mass of arms generated by the war and supplied by speculators and profiteers, individual and national, outside the country. Moreover it would accustom the people to the use of force in the solution of social and political problems.

> Militarist entrepreneurs and multiple dictatorships: this is bound to be the legacy of a war which is conducted on the present terms. The vacuum in the ethical base—for national boundary is neither an ethical nor an ideological base for any conflict—this vacuum will be filled by a new military ethic—coercion. [53]

In Soyinka's view the war, instead of resolving the problems of ethnic rivalry and institutionalised corruption, intensified both.

> The war means a consolidation of crime, an acceptance of the scale of values that created the conflict, indeed an allegiance and enshrinement of that scale of values because it is now intimately bound to the sense of national identity. [54]

Despite the Federal victory the issue of unity still remains. And the process of national reconstruction has again involved attempts to solve this most intractable problem. In 1967 General Gowon had reduced Ironsi's twenty-one Provinces to twelve States. In the latest reorganisation under Lieutenant-General Obasanjo in 1976 the number has been increased to nineteen, in a division ironically similar to that of Ironsi. With the breaking up of the monolithic Regions it is hoped that a greater sense of national identity will emerge. Ethnic tensions still abound however. A tendency towards a localised micro-

33

nationalism *within* the states has already been remarked. Professor S. Aluko describes what he calls 'statism',[55] a prejudice which ensures that all important posts within a state not under the control of the Federal Government are given only to natives of that state. The answer to such problems can only come with time; with the extension of Federal authority, with greater regional mobility and the improvement of education. An encouraging development here is the introduction in 1978 of a new, unified entry system for the universities, whereby a large proportion of students will be placed in universities outside their ethnic homeland.[56] The difficulties at all levels are nevertheless great, and prospects for real national unity and a healthy national culture seem still uncertain.

## Politics and politicians

All over Africa in the years following independence the multi-party parliamentary systems hastily set up by the departing British or French have given way to 'one party' states or to military dictatorships. This breakdown has been said in Europe to prove that 'the blacks were not ready for democracy' and are incapable of the political discretion and moderation shown by Europeans. The first part of this proposition seems undeniable; but to attribute this unreadiness to the supposed inferiority of Africans to Europeans is naive. The most superficial analysis shows that, in Nigeria and elsewhere in Africa, both history and economics conspire to render parliamentary democracy in the European sense unworkable. To begin with there is no history of any such system in the ex-colonies. In traditional society authority was either autocratic or communal and thus quite alien to European pluralism, while the colonial administration was an authoritarian bureaucracy which tended to treat political opposition as sedition. Ruth First comments drily on the claims of Britain and France to have 'prepared' their colonies for independence.

34

If there was any training and adaptation before independence, it was a schooling in the bureaucratic toils of colonial government, a preparation not for independence, but against it. [57]

History had thus given the new nations no experience of the parliamentary politics of office and opposition. K.A. Busia, a member of the Ghanaian opposition during the rule of Nkrumah, complains feelingly about the British assumption that a kind of 'instant' parliamentary democracy could succeed upon independence.

The British teach that an opposition is an essential part of the parliamentary democratic system; yet their policy for helping the institution of the parliamentary system at this final stage never included any official help to the opposition. [58]

As Busia indicates, in the years immediately preceding independence the chief concern of the colonial government was to ensure 'stability', which invariably meant attempting to entrench in authority a strong and 'reliable' leader or group (in the case of Nigeria, the North), while paying lip-service to the democratic balance of government and opposition. Neither the traditional nor the colonial background then lend much support to parliamentary democracy in Africa.

There are also deeper social reasons for its lack of success. Since the formation of modern socio-economic classes is, as we have seen, at such an early stage in most African countries, the bases on which European political parties are founded have so far been lacking. Only the bourgeoisie possesses sufficient class-solidarity to act as a purposive political force. And, as Peil has shown in the case of Nigeria, awareness of the very real conflicts of interest between this class and the populace as a whole is as yet largely stifled by traditional allegiances. While government is still viewed by many people not as a policy-making body accountable directly to the electorate, but in terms inherited from traditional or colonial rule. In much of Africa then political parties appeal not to ideology or class-interest, but to traditional ethnic or religious loyalties, the class-interest they serve being in every case that of the bourgeoisie. A tiny minority within the educated elite

35

may see politics in more 'modern' terms. Max and Odili in Achebe's *A Man of the People*, with their catastrophic progressive political party, certainly do. But, as they themselves acknowledge, they are divorced from society as a whole. The result of this confused situation has been that following independence most African nations have abandoned the pretence of European party-politics and adopted some system of government more in accord with their own particular history and traditions. In the fortunate (at least in this respect) case of Tanzania, where the 1961 elections gave every parliamentary seat but one to the Tanganyika African National Union, the new 'one-party' government has easily taken the place of the traditional communal authority. Elsewhere ethnic rivalries prove intractable. One group takes power at the expense of another, as in Smith's Rhodesia or Amin's Uganda; or as in Kenya and Nigeria, uneasy compromises are made between traditional rivals. And quite often the internal strains become so great that the army steps in to restore order and civilian rule is abruptly ended.

It seems that the first prime minister of the Nigerian Federation, Alhaji Sir Abubakar Tafawa Balewa, was hoping for a variation of the 'one-party' system in his country, by which the North would retain permanent domination of the coalition government. In an interview given early in 1966 he is reported to have said: 'A political opposition in the Western accepted sense is a luxury that we cannot afford.'[59] Thus does entrenched authority justify its power in terms of the preservation of stability and national unity against ideological attack. And his words sound heavily ironic in view of the fact that he was assassinated within days of making this remark. However, there is an essential truth in what he said. There did not exist in Nigeria at that time, and could scarcely have existed, a political opposition in the 'Western accepted' sense, (although this was scarcely because Nigeria could not 'afford' such a 'luxury'). Indeed, as if to prove this point, the Prime Minister's assassins showed themselves to lack any power base in effective political organisation or mass support when their *coup* failed to become the 'people's uprising' hoped for by Soyinka. And *within* the established political elite no group possessed sufficient ideological coherence to constitute a principled 'opposition' in the true sense of the word. There are particular Nigerian reasons for this lack of real political debate. The West African climate for instance had always inhibited the growth of a large white settler population such as complicated and 'politicised' the transfer of power from white to black in Kenya, Zimbabwe and Algeria. There had never been the wholesale dispossession of the peasantry which took place in Kenya, and which forms the background of Ngugi's novel, *A Grain of Wheat* (1967). Political opposition to the colonist was never compelled to take the form of a mass movement or a protracted armed struggle. There was never any real Nigerian equivalent to Mau Mau or the Patriotic Front with their ideological leaders and apologists. The educated intellectual was not forced by repression to find common cause with the mass of the people, and independence took the form of an unusually smooth transfer of power from a small white elite to a small black elite. The consequence has been a lack of politicisation among the people as a whole and the elite in particular. Both before and after independence the Nigerian elite and the political parties which emerged from within it lacked both ideological complexity and identification with the people as a whole.

Worse still, the parties, lacking any national ideology or power base, were driven to find their identity in terms of the regional groupings within the nation, for which they rapidly became the mouthpieces. The NCNC (National Council of Nigeria and the Cameroons, later, National Council of Nigerian Citizens), the earliest political party to be founded, performed at first the function of *the* nationalist anti-colonial party. And had the geo-ethnic complexities of Nigeria been less than they were it might have dominated post-colonial Nigeria as TANU does Tanzania or the CPP did Ghana in its early years. However, by the late 1940s it was apparent that the NCNC could never become a 'national' party of that kind. It was closely identified with its leader, Nnamdi Azikiwe, an Ibo; and once Chief Awolowo had founded the Action Group in

37

the Western Region (significantly as an offshoot of a Yoruba cultural society, the Egbe Omo Oduduwa[60]) it became clear that—as might indeed be expected in the Nigerian situation—each major ethnic group would have its own political party. In the North, political organisation tended to be even more ethnically monolithic than in the Southern regions, with the Islamic religion acting as a strong unifying force. The very name of the Northern party, the Northern People's Congress, and its motto, 'One North, One Nation', pointed to its regional base. Southerners indeed were not permitted to be members.

The period of civilian rule from 1960-6 then shows not so much a failure of the Westminster parliamentary system (which never really existed) as the successive rise and fall of different coalitions of ethnic groups, led by members of the new bourgeoisie or of the Northern obligarchy. It was not so much a case of conflicting political ideologies or socio-economic classes, as of conflicting regional interests and also, to a large extent, of conflicting personalities. There is little sign of politics in the most respectable sense of the term, but a great deal of politicking. Within each party the pattern is very similar. At the top, eager to profit from the spoils of de-colonisation, are members of the Southern bourgeoisie and the entrenched traditional rulers of the North. These leaders are supported by a largely peasant electorate whose loyalty is based on ethnic identity reinforced by religion or the dis-tribution of largesse. The instability of this situation is due in part to the lack of a place within it for anything resembling the 'loyal opposition' essential to any stable party system. Loyalty is to one's easily identifiable ethnic group rather than to the elusive abstraction 'Nigeria'. The other groups are 'enemies'. The result is that defeat in an election, instead of being the sobering and salutary lesson for the loser which it is conventionally held to be in a stable democracy, is an un-mitigated catastrophe. The European convention, whereby office and opposition alternate between parties, relies on two important principles. Firstly, the interest that all parties share in keeping the system intact must at all times outweigh the

38

interest any one of them has in victory over any particular policy. Secondly there must be an accepted part to be played in government or public life by the members of the parties which lose elections. In Nigeria in the 1960s these principles failed to operate. Loyalty to the central state and to the parliamentary system was weaker than loyalty to the ethnically based party. And the winning of an election was a signal for the victor to reward supporters wholesale, and punish opponents.

The problem was compounded by the nation's poverty and lack of development. As in most third-world countries there are in Nigeria few sources of wealth or social prestige outside the control of the government. In a developed Western nation, with its painfully evolved checks and balances, an opposition party still has its part to play within the system, or its members may play prominent roles in independent industry and commerce. In an underdeveloped country, lacking such political and economic diversification, the winning party as it were 'sweeps the board', and all avenues of advancement are monopolised by its own supporters. It is for this reason that, following elections in underdeveloped nations, so many members of opposition parties cross the floor to join the majority party. Political power is the prime avenue to economic power. It is for this reason also that elections, and even censuses (upon the results of which numbers of parliamentary seats are allocated to different areas) have been in Nigeria so marred by the sort of corruption portrayed in Achebe's *A Man of the People*. No party can afford to lose, at any price; and any means is fair against the ethno-political enemy. This habit of mind renders debate on policies between opposing parties almost meaningless; reducing it to strings of abuse and extravagant promises in identical form from all sides. Nor, it is to be feared, is this state of affairs greatly changed even when political parties are separated from ethnicity. The ideological vacuum within the new Southern bourgeois elite and the educational backwardness of the North still militate against real politics. It may be feared indeed that the recent attempts in Nigeria to detribalise politics by stipulating proven multi-ethnic composition in every party's national officers, may simply ensure that the *only* motive for going into politics will now be pure venality.

A fuller idea of the nature and tone of political life in Nigeria before the military takeover in 1966 can be obtained by examining the ventures into literature made by three of the most prominent politicians of the time, each of whom has published an autobiography in which he explains his beliefs and political philosophy. *My Life* (1962) by Alhaji Sir Ahmadu Bello, Premier of the Northern Region from 1954 until his assassination in the *coup* of January 1966, requires separate treatment because of its Islamic and Northern perspective. The other two: *Awo* (1960), by Chief Obafemi Awolowo, Premier of the Western Region from 1954 until 1962, and *My Odyssey* (1970), by Dr Nnamdi Azikiwe, an Easterner and first President of the Nigerian Federation (from 1963 until 1966), may be treated together. Both men share the characteristic perspectives of the new Southern (Christian) educated elite.

Ahmadu Bello held by right of descent the traditional title, Sardauna of Sokoto (originally 'Captain of the Sultan's Bodyguard'), and traced his ancestry back to Shehu Usman dan Fodio, leader of the Fulani *jihad* which swept across central West Africa in the early nineteenth century. His attitudes are thus those of a ruler established by traditional right and by divine will. In this of course he differs fundamentally from the ruling members of the Southern elite, whose right to power is 'political' in a more modern sense, deriving from elections working upon recently established democratic principles. Bello refers with dignified distaste to 'the Southern politicians' and at times seems to feel the term demeaning when applied to the Northern rulers. His perspective makes no distinction between the religious and the political. From early in his autobiography the hand of God is to be seen.

Some of the children died, but though I was sick from time to time God's destiny lay before me and I was brought through it.[61]

And for Bello even elections, usually thought of as expressions of the will of the people, owe their legitimacy to a higher authority: 'God willed that I should be elected'.[62] As we shall see, the Southern politicians express similar gratitude to God for their success, but with something of that routine conventionality which is familiar in modern Christianity. Ahmadu Bello's faith is more intense and pervasive. At times it gives him an aloof indifference to politics and political debate. Take for example this comment on a speech made by one of his political opponents, advocating an early date for independence.

> It was good oratory and he never missed a point, but did he really gain anything? I wonder. The hand of God was moving as always, using us men as its pieces on the wide field of the world events. Nothing which we could have said or done would have moved the date of Independence forward, or put it back a single hour from the moment in which it was ordained from the dawn of time itself.[63]

To the certainties which Bello derives from his religion is added the confidence of the aristocrat born to power. He is of a profoundly conservative cast of mind and views government always in terms of the imposition of 'discipline' from above, never in terms of balances of interest or popular consensus. He is unable to conceive of any conflict between the interest of himself and his fellow rulers on the one hand and that of the people as a whole on the other. He is an authoritarian patrician. Although he expresses approval of elections and increased 'democracy', he clearly envisages the process very much on his own terms. He remarks for instance on the disadvantages of elected councils, which if they are 'bad' are so much more difficult to dismiss than a single chief, especially if, as happened on one occasion, such a council represents a town containing 'large numbers of strangers and travellers'.[64] (Bello several times warns of the danger to order presented by 'strangers' who, it is implied, corrupt the Northern people with alien ideas.) In the case of the particular council to which he refers, indecisiveness and inefficiency may well have been the reasons for its dismissal. But other, more political sources of conflict between an hereditary ruler and the elected representatives of the people,

41

may arise. Bello shows no awareness of this possibility and assumes that the people need no defence against their rulers. His characteristic approach to the problems of government can be seen in the following passage:

> The Bornu people are the hardest in the country to administer, but we always find that if the Shehu is left to 'have his head' he will usually bring things through all right. Some British officers could not understand this, simple as it is. . . [65]

Along with this stress on authority goes a strong dislike of social change. *My Life* recounts a constant struggle to maintain stability and continuity against disruption and degeneration. Although he recognises the benefits of progress, he judges the present always in relation to the Fulani greatness of the nineteenth century and the stability of the colonial period. He sees the granting of Regional 'self-government' to the North in 1959 as

> the restoration of the pre-1900 era, modernised, polished, democratised, refined, but not out of recognition; reconstructed, but still within the same framework and on the same foundations; comprehensible by all and appreciated by all. [66]

And he warns against any attempt to endanger the prestige of the emirs, even by removing their traditional trappings. This he insists would 'set the country back for years, and indeed, were such changes to be drastic, it might well need another Lugard to pull things together again'. [67]

The typical Northern combination of Islamic faith and conservatism which Bello exemplifies holds unfortunate implications for relations between the North and the rest of Nigeria. It is quite clear from *My Life* that if the prophecy that the Fulani would 'dip the Holy Koran in the sea' [68] had been fulfilled, the North would now, in one of Bello's favourite phrases, be 'running its own show'. He candidly concedes that it is only the South's control over access to the sea which prevented the North going its separate way in the early 1950s. [69] The word 'country' is used in his book to signify the North as often as it signifies Nigeria as a whole. His fear of the South is of course only too well grounded. It is impossible not to agree with him that had Independence been rushed through in the 1950s under pressure from the Southern politicians, and on their terms, the North would have suffered considerably. Bello feelingly complains of the insensitivity of the Southerners at the 1953 London Conference to the fact that 'we, the NPC, had the most to lose if things went wrong'.[70] However Bello's attitude to all non-Northern ideas and viewpoints shows a lack of sympathy or even interest, which goes far beyond this immediate political issue and gives some insight into the more fundamental problem. It is quite clear that despite his usual politeness, he views all 'alien' culture, religion and art, whether African or European, with total indifference, or in some cases contempt. The social scene in the South, particularly Lagos with its 'thugs' and 'riff-raff', he finds distressingly uncomfortable.

> We all found it very strange and did not care for our stays in Lagos. The whole place was alien to our ideas of life and we found that the Members [of the House of Representatives] for the other Regions might well belong to another world so far as we are concerned.[71]

This is not a surprising reaction when one considers that Bello did not travel outside the North of Nigeria until he was in his late thirties.

These limitations mean that Bello is unwilling or unable to understand the feelings and motives of people from different backgrounds from himself. And his views on important political issues are consequently startlingly simple and dogmatic. The views of his political opponents for instance are never seriously analysed or countered. They are simply dismissed. The Northern Elements Progressive Union (a small Northern radical party) he states briskly 'had different views from ours on the future of the Native Authorities—largely due to faulty understanding and personal experiences'.[72] Such attacks on political opponents may perhaps be expected to lack complexity. But a wider analysis shows that Bello's political perceptions *never* go any further than this. He never discusses any political problem on both sides, he never sees any issue as a clash between equally understandable ideals or

43

interpretations of the facts. The Northern ruling-class view, which he expounds, is invariably right, and those who oppose it are contemptible fools or rowdy troublemakers. His approach to 'the so-called minorities question' shows him in characteristic high-handed, contemptuous vein:

> The most embarrassing Commission was the one on the Minorities. This wandered round the country listening patiently to scores upon scores of people who thought, for one reason or another, that their area should be carved out of the Region in which it then lay . . .
> There were three groups which made the most noise . . .
> I have given this problem the closest consideration for years and am forced to the conclusion that there is nothing in it beyond the personal aggrandisement of its leaders and a desire to embarrass us.[73]

His conclusive point against the Middle-Belt claim to autonomy (he does not concern himself with the minorities in the other Regions) is an appeal to the historical rule of his ancestors over their territory.

> It must never be forgotten that almost the whole of the Region as it is today, and a great deal outside it, was ruled by my great-great-grandfather's family through their Lieutenants or by the great Shehus of Bornu . . .[74]

A similar limitation reveals itself in his comments on the position of women. The genealogy which prefaces *My Life* contains no female name; the chapter entitled 'My Family' also makes no mention of any woman: and most surprising of all, this autobiography lacks any reference to its author's wives. With so strongly patriarchal a perspective it is scarcely surprising that his attitude to the question of votes for women is one of bewildered incomprehension. He quite honestly cannot see why anyone should think it an important issue.

> We are often taken to task about votes for women. The Eastern and Western Regions have given their women the vote . . . I agree that no particular harm has been done, though I must claim that no outstanding good has come of it. I daresay that we shall introduce it in the end here, but . . .[75]

Understandably perhaps, Bello's attitudes and those of the other Northern rulers frequently led to frustration and exasperation on the part of their political opponents. Bello's response to this always possessed the dignity and control of the born aristocrat. In *My Life* he often leaves aside the particular point at issue in order to lament the 'rudeness' and bad manners of his adversaries. [76] In a personal aside he even associates the largeness of mind to which he attributes his self-control with his large physical size.

> Being a big man myself, I find that I can get on with big men better than I can with small ones—but I must draw a certain line, for the big men must have big minds. I have no use for men who are merely big and I have no use at all for people who are stupid and I seem to be forced to come up against numbers of them. [77]

It was fortunate for relations between the North and Britain that during the last days of colonial rule the Commonwealth Secretaries, Lennox Boyd and Lord Chandos were both 'big' men.

The most striking difference between the views of Bello and those not only of Southerners within Nigeria but also of virtually all other leaders of colonised peoples, lies in his almost unqualified admiration for the colonist. Lugard's policy of 'Indirect Rule' was very much to the advantage of the Northern rulers, and moreover the ideology of the authoritarian British administration largely coincided with their own. From Bello's point of view then the British were 'the instrument of destiny and were fulfilling the will of God. In their way they did it well.' He stresses their 'politeness' during the early days of colonialism. They were he says 'obviously out to help us rather than themselves'. [78] (Throughout the book the pronouns 'we' and 'us' serve to imply the unity of all Northerners.) Even after Independence Bello expresses himself eager to employ expatriates in the Northern administration. As far as he is concerned they are clearly preferable to troublesome educated Southerners, and they facilitate control from the top. Bello's attitude towards the British is always explicable, as here, in the light of the danger from the South. The British

45

offer themselves as natural allies against domination.

> You will see that we were never militant 'nationalists' as some were.
> We were sure that in God's good time we would get the power. The
> British had promised this frequently and we were content to rest on
> these promises . . . [79]

Such remarks as this make it easy to see why Southerners
accused the North of allowing themselves to be 'used' by the
British. Allowing themselves to be so used however was in
fact to their advantage. Characteristically Bello does not see
this alliance in terms of political expediency. It is a matter of
personal respect between Northern rulers and British rulers.
'We talked the same language' he says, and adds with a certain
innocence of political realities: 'But so could the Southern
parties if they had wanted to.'[80] As far as Bello is concerned
it is the common values of politeness, dignity and respect for
tradition which draw Northerners and the British together. It
is significant in this respect that one of the most glowing
passages in *My Life* relates the visit of the Queen to Northern
Nigeria in 1956. Because, of course, despite all the differences,
Bello's power derives its legitimacy from exactly the same
principles as that of the British Queen: descent from ancient
warlords and the grace of God. It is thus understandable that
he should welcome his fellow ruler with unusual consideration
and respect. He even detects the divine element in her royalty
at work among the populace.

> Incidentally, it is interesting to note that during the whole period of
> the Queen's visit in the North, no cases of crime were reported to
> the police in the places she was visiting . . . It seemed as though a
> kind of peace, not of this world, came over the country . . . [81]

To turn to the autobiographies of the two Southern
politicians is to enter a different world, and one with more
familiar perspectives to the observer of de-colonisation.
Despite the manifold differences between Awolowo and
Azikiwe, they share many of the assumptions and ideals
characteristic of the early stages of anti-colonial nationalism.
In many ways they seem to be opposites, and indeed for

much of their careers a purely personal rivalry between them
has marked their public lives. Their educational backgrounds
account for some differences. Azikiwe went to the United
States at the age of twenty-one and has retained something
of the brash, entrepreneurial *élan* of the American ethos.
Awolowo on the other hand remained in Nigeria until he was
thirty-five years old, when he went to study law in London.
He is a more abstemious, even austere character; if equally
strong-willed. Azikiwe's energies have been devoted to
building up a huge business empire; while Awolowo, though
also a successful businessman, is most respected as a lawyer
and for the administrative efficiency and dynamism which he
brought to the affairs of the Western Region during his period
as Premier. Politically Azikiwe tended at first to favour
centralisation of government, whereas Awolowo advocated
devolution. Considering all these differences, and the hard
words they have to say about each other, the profound ideological similarity which reveals itself in their autobiographies
is the more remarkable. And an examination of the qualities
and attitudes which they have in common will throw the
clearest light on the political tone of the Southern elite
during the last years of colonialism and the First Republic.

Their most striking common characteristic is the strong
flavour of the 'self-made man' about their personalities and
opinions. Both of them experienced immense difficulty in
finding the resources to pursue their educational ambitions,
and their sense of personal achievement is therefore high.
They each attribute their ultimate success in life to a home-
spun personal philosophy, sometimes patched together from
rather miscellaneous sources. Azikiwe makes a great deal of
the essential part that sport and good-sportsmanship have
played in his career, one of the chapters of his autobiography,
*My Odyssey* being devoted to 'Our Activities in Sport' (the
plural signifies all the members of his business organisations).
Life he tells us, in the familiar words of generations of English
and American schoolmasters, is like a race.

Athletics makes the average young man realise that life is a race

47

in which all must start at the scratch. At the shot of the starter's gun, some runners will rush at a blind speed as a cyclone. Their cyclonic start is a fair prediction of a cyclonic fadeout. Some runners will run impulsively in a lackadaisical manner . . . Some runners are methodical in the way they run. They plan the varying stages of their race: the time to set a fast pace, the time to let down a bit imperceptibly, the time to accelerate the pace . . .

These tricks of running have influenced my way of life . . . [82]

Chief Awolowo in *Awo* derives his philosophy from an anthology of 'terse, powerful articles' taken from the English patriotic magazine *John Bull*, entitled *The Human Machine*, and a book, significantly entitled *It's Up To You*, 'written, if I remember rightly, by an American author'. Awolowo comments: 'The philosophy of the latter book is very simple but also very true and fundamental'. It is expressed in an allegory concerning large and small beans in a jar which is shaken, 'and, behold! the small beans rattle to the bottom and the big beans shake to the top', the moral being that 'Nobody can fool the jar of life'. (Having tested this observation I can testify to its accuracy, at least as far as beans are concerned.) Merit, allegorised as the large beans, will inevitably find its way to the top, while the 'small' in mind or morals will sink to the bottom.

The *sine qua non* for anyone who wants to get to the top, therefore, is to increase his size and weight in his particular calling—that is mentally, professionally, morally, and spiritually. [83]

Like Ahmadu Bello, neither Azikiwe nor Awolowo allow much part in their success to accidents of history or to luck. Their achievement is due to their own endeavours in the race of life or their own weight in the jar of life. Personal virtue, uprightness and of course the approval of God, have seen them through. As Awolowo remarks:

I do not hesitate to confess that I owe my success in life to three factors: the Grace of God, a spartan self-discipline, and a good wife. [84]

The contrast such homely, 'pithy' philosophies of life present

48

with the expressions of ideology to be found even in the more informal works of such other African political leaders as Tom Mboya, Julius Nyerere or even Kwame Nkrumah, is striking. As a recipe for the advancement of society as a whole both Azikiwe and Awolowo emphasise the role of personal self-improvement and favour the ample rewarding of 'merit', by which they mean the attributes that brought them their own success. They are both unashamed elitists in this respect. Azikiwe expresses his belief in an 'aristocracy of intelligence',[85] while Awolowo's early political aims, expressed in the Nigerian Youth Charter of 1938, include a demand for 'better pay for Africans in the civil service—*particularly* in the clerical and less subordinate branches'[86] (my italics). It seems then that in the case of both men the consequence of their intense personal struggles to better themselves is a conviction that what society needs is more opportunities for young men and women to travel the same road. Both *My Odyssey* and *Awo* are explicitly presented as models for aspiring youth to follow, the implication being that the most urgent need in modern African society is a greater supply of aggressive self-made millionaires—a view which would not be shared by many observers.

In their conceptions of the role of the indigenous politician in Nigeria before and after independence Azikiwe and Awolowo show a characteristic commonsense pragmatism. The young Azikiwe (understandably) saw it as his first task in life to make himself rich. Then, adopting for himself the role hitherto monopolised by the all-dispensing colonial power, he would bestow his patronage on others. In a 'solemn vow' made while he was unemployed in the United States on the last day of 1937, he pledged:

> Thirdly, that, henceforth, I shall utilise my earned income to secure my enjoyment of a high standard of living and also to give a helping hand to the needy. [87]

Elsewhere he remarks 'the role of a Good Samaritan appealed to me'.[88] His aim, which of course he amply realised, was to become a wealthy philanthropist, and his conception of his political role was essentially as an extension of such philanthropy. There is no hint of moral uneasiness about the system by which such vast wealth can be accumulated in private hands. Expressed in terms of political theory this is close to the eighteenth-century doctrine that the rich are a boon to society since their superfluity supports the poor, who would otherwise starve. Awolowo expresses himself with similar forthrightness about his own personal ambitions in the letter he wrote to Mr Ernest Ikoli on 21st November 1943 concerning his 'private plan' of life. He intended, he explained, to 'hibernate' from politics for four years.

> In that time I was going 'to make myself formidable intellectually', 'morally invulnerable', 'to make all the money that is possible for a man with my brains and brawn to make in Nigeria', and 'to acquire a profession'. 'After getting this profession,' I added, and as it turned out, prophetically, 'I should like to make more money. That may take another five years. Then I shall start a new offensive.' [89]

It is to be noted that the profession (the law was the one chosen) is an asset, to be 'acquired' or 'got', as a means of making money and eventually thereby gaining political power.

In view of this personalisation of Nigerian politics it is scarcely surprising that the remarks of both Azikiwe and Awolowo on broader political principles and ideals are extremely cautious and uncommitted. Commitment to larger causes counts for little when personal ambition is the prime political motive. Unusually among black African states Nigeria has produced no ideologists of distinction, no significant advocate for instance of any form of 'African socialism'. Azikiwe's remarks on socialism and capitalism in *My Odyssey* are of truly Byzantine subtlety.

> I decided that to be a wage-earner for life was to perpetuate that phase of capitalism which was obnoxious, and thought that by becoming a small capitalist I might show by example that, with its faults, capitalism was only a means to a happy life and it was an institution which was necessary in man's economic evolution. Some of these views are still the basis of my economic philosophy, but others have been radically modified since I studied the ideology of

socialism. I have to admit that the capitalist system is a universal practice in Africa and, until it is universally rejected or radically modified, the prudent thing to do is to adapt ourselves to it until a revolution has taken place which might transform Africa or the world into a socialist leviathan. [90]

This interesting argument deserves detailed analysis, not least for its complex use of the resources of English syntax. Azikiwe tells us that he decided to be a capitalist rather than a wage-earner because to be a wage-earner was to promote 'that phase of capitalism which was obnoxious'. (Which phase is that, one wonders? ) It cannot but be suspected however that it is his own *personal* position as a wage-earner which is obnoxious to him, rather than the phenomenon of wage-earning itself, since his solution—to become an employer of wage-earners himself—seems an odd way of striking a blow against the wage-earning system. His purpose however in becoming 'a small capitalist' (he is generally considered to be a millionaire) is to show by example that capitalism is not an end in itself, but only a means to a happy life. Although whether he means a happy life for the capitalist or for the wage-earner is not clear. And how is this life of 'example' to be distinguished by the world at large from the unexemplary lives of less purely motivated capitalists? —by philanthropy presumably. But now it emerges that, after all, the institution of capitalism (some other 'phase' of it perhaps? ) is not in fact obnoxious, but 'necessary in man's economic evolution'. The capitalist is absolved. We are then informed that the views summarised so far are still the basis of Azikiwe's philosophy— but not all of them. Some of his early views have been radically modified by his study of socialism. Unfortunately he omits to tell us which these are, or how they have been modified. At any rate, one thing is clear. It is as a capitalist that Azikiwe will prudently remain until the capitalist system is 'universally rejected', at which time, it seems, he will reveal himself a true socialist at heart and take his well-earned place in the socialist leviathan. His conception of the revolution which is to bring this socialist world into existence seems a strangely disembodied one however, for a former lecturer in

51

history and political science at Howard University. Socialism will (or 'might') somehow suddenly occur, without millionaire capitalists like himself being involved in the process one way or the other. Upon which he will 'adapt' to it, in the same way one presumes as he previously adapted to capitalism. The fact that millionaires owe their existence to a constant and systematic suppression of any movement towards socialism seems to have escaped his attention. One may be inclined to wonder whether his analysis in this passage really goes any deeper than the ingenuous remark of the Ghanaian millionaire, Krobo Edusei: 'Socialism doesn't mean that if you've made a lot of money, you can't keep it.' [91]

Awolowo's attitude towards socialism has far greater intellectual coherence, but is also tentative and qualified. As one might expect from what has been said so far, he has a healthy suspicion of the restraints which some socialist regimes place on the economic and social liberty of the individual. He expresses a generalised approval of 'Western' values, particularly the freedom of the individual. He declares 'my preference is unhesitatingly and unequivocally for the Western democracies'[92] over the communist states, because of their freedom of speech and open government. He has no patience with theories of one-party rule:

> Democracy and a one party system of government are in my opinion, mutually exclusive. [93]

Nevertheless he considers himself a socialist—but a strictly democratic one:

> 'I and most of my colleagues are democrats by nature, and socialists by conviction.' [94]

He appears in fact as a typical moderate social democrat of the European pattern, believing in limited public ownership and central planning in government, but always alert to individual and minority rights. These general expressions of belief may seem a little disembodied and second-hand in the context of the Nigeria of 1960. But it is when one turns to his treatment of specific Nigerian issues, such as the resistance of the Western Region to Federal interference from the centre, that one begins to see the relevance of his social democratic theory to political realities. Moreover he also places the question of ideology within the larger context of the post-colonial world. Like Mboya in Kenya he is too aware of the pressures from the developed West to feel that socialism in anything but a modified and compromised sense is possible in his country. And in any case he is more concerned with immediate practicalities than in taking ideological positions.

> The emphasis, as far as I am concerned, has always been on the words 'expedient and effective'. From time to time, the point has been keenly urged by a very influential body of people in the party that the Action Group should declare itself a socialist party. My own view, which is shared by many, is that what matters is not the label which a party bears, but the policy which it actually pursues either in office or opposition. In any case, in the circumstances of Nigeria, it would be reckless and lead to economic chaos to adopt a rigid socialist policy, or drink the cup of undiluted capitalism. For the rapid development of our country, we need foreign capital as well as managerial and technical know-how. At the same time, the admission of foreign capital into the country must be well-regulated . . . [95]

These sentiments could have come from a speech by Mboya, and express excellently the moderate 'realistic' approach to the post-colonial problem.

Despite the interest of Awolowo's views on economic strategy however, it is not for its political analyses that *Awo* is memorable; its vitality comes always from the personality of the author himself. In this it is similar to *My Odyssey*. Although autobiographers may be expected to be egocentric, these authors are so with a peculiarly Nigerian inflection and intensity. There is a close, almost unconscious, identification of their own personal interest with that of their entire people. Their sense that their own individual fortunes are also those of the nation as a whole is remarkable. Perhaps it is not surprising that in the social and moral vacuum between traditional and modern which we have seen in Nigeria, the private aims of the dynamic and ambitious citizen should easily take on the appearance of the public good. Both Azikiwe and

53

Awolowo feel that their own personal aggrandisement is somehow *in itself* an aggrandisement of Nigeria, and in a sense they may be right. When Awolowo wrote to a millionaire (unnamed) asking for an interest-free loan to help him to 'acquire a profession' he showed no embarrassment in representing his own interests as those of his nation:

> ... by helping me to achieve my ambition you are indirectly or even directly helping Nigeria or even Africa ...
> God and Africa will be grateful to you for ever and ever. [96]

And although Azikiwe reports his prayers to God for Christian humility in using his wealth only for the good of Nigeria as a whole, he sees no contradiction between this and his first priority which, as we have seen, was to achieve 'my enjoyment of a high standard of living'.

It is this high self-regard and lack of self-doubt which must be responsible, at least in part, for the inflation of style which marks both books, but particularly *My Odyssey*. Such inflation is a characteristic feature of much Nigerian English and is a favourite object of satire for such novelists as T.M. Aluko and Chinua Achebe. There are other reasons however for such stylistic flamboyance. Ali Mazrui has commented on the importance of oratory to the modern African politician whose constituents are accustomed to the oral proverbs and riddles of a pre-literate culture. Mazrui traces the inflation of political language in Africa in the 1950s and 1960s to the desire of the politicians to give the impression of Western learning or 'book' in terms comprehensible to such an audience.

> Words ending with *-ization* or *-ism* could send an audience into ecstasy if enough of them were used near together to create an impression of massive verbal power. It might even be said that while literary quotations were the functional equivalent of proverbs, the real functional equivalents of riddles were long English words.[97]

Naturally enough such verbal habits spill over from the politicians' speeches into their writing. Azikiwe in particular frequently employs quotations from British or American authors. Ahmadu Bello rebuked the Southern politicians for this particular affectation:

> I have wondered why some Southern members are so fond of quotations: surely if a thing is worth saying it is better put in one's own words?[98]

Bello's own traditional authority requires measured composure of manner rather than vigorous persuasion, and *his* audience is suspicious rather than enthusiastic about Western education. Consequently his style is usually plain and unremarkable. Both Awolowo and Azikiwe on the other hand lapse at times into over-literariness. Awolowo occasionally affects archaic poeticism.

> ... sans my father, sans my mother, and sans the happy atmosphere of my home at Ikenne...
> So Mote It Be.
> Besides I was already engaged to a beautiful damsel whom I planned to marry by the end of 1937. [99]

It is perhaps unfair to stress this aspect of *Awo*, whose *basic* style is businesslike and unaffected. The style of *My Odyssey*, however, whose title indicates the author's conception of his heroic role, reflects a sublime pretension. Its tone may be illustrated by the opening paragraph.

> My life is a pilgrimage from the unknown to the unknown. I do not know whence I emanated or whither I am bound. I have been taught that my father and mother were biologically concerned with my conception and birth, during which process I developed as an embryo, emerged as a helpless baby, evolved into a dependent adolescent, and grew up into an independent man. After this evolution, I learned that idealism is that aspect of philosophy which concerns itself always with standards of perfection; while materialism reasons that, since the facts of the universe are sufficiently explained by the existence and nature of matter, so the material well-being of the individual should determine the code of human conduct. [100]

The long account of the author's lineage which follows (employing the biblical 'begat' at one point) and the reference to the comet which was reported to have signalised his birth,

55

may seem mere exuberance or perhaps intentionally droll. But as the narrative unfolds the fundamental gravity which underlies its gusto, reveals itself. The effect of mock-heroic is quite unintentional: in the summaries prefixed to each chapter, for instance:

*My struggles in 'God's Country' among godly and godless images of God.*

*My baptism in the furnace of imperialism by descendants of Boadicea in the land of yellow metal.* [The Gold Coast.]

*How I made honest efforts to protect my newspaper ventures from the pitfalls of human frailty and yet they succumbed to the irony of fate and the will of constituted authority.* [101]

Throughout the book the author's sense of his high destiny inbues the style with an elevation which dignifies even the most unpromising material. At one point, out of work in the United States and desperate for money, the young Azikiwe is offered a job as a blackleg working in a mine at wages artificially inflated by the employer's desire to break a strike. Quite naturally, and without any sense of incongruity, he sees the dilemma in terms of Hamlet's meditation on whether or not to commit suicide.

> I remembered the soliloquy of Hamlet, whom the immortal Shakespeare made to ruminate:
> 'To be or not to be, that is the question:
> Whether 'tis nobler in the mind to suffer
> The slings and arrows of outrageous fortune,
> Or to take arms against a sea of troubles
> And, by opposing end them? . . .'
> I argued with myself that, if I did not work, I would be without funds . . . I had suffered 'the slings and arrows of outrageous fortune'. It was time for me 'to take arms against a sea of troubles and, by opposing, end them'. So I decided to go ahead and do the job, and face the consequences of my decision. [102]

The moral, political and literary attitudes revealed in this passage are highly characteristic. And one is tempted to detect a 'typically Nigerian' inflection in its brisk, unembarrassed pragmatism.

# 2 Literature and the politics of language

## European languages in Africa

There are compelling reasons why the languages of the former colonial powers, English, French and Portuguese, continue to be used in independent African states. With the present political and economic strength of France and of the English-speaking nations, the retention of their languages for diplomacy and commerce is clearly a great advantage to a newly independent state. While in literature the use of such widespread languages gives access to the widest audiences. Internal factors may be equally important. The ethnic and linguistic diversity within many African states makes the use of the colonial language in education and in public life a simple political necessity. Several hundred languages are spoken, for example, within the border arbitrarily bequeathed to Nigeria by its colonial history.[1] In such a country to speak or write in one's native tongue is to reach only a limited audience. Even a speaker using one of the three languages officially termed 'major' will remain incomprehensible to large numbers of his or her fellow Nigerians. Moreover, different languages usually belong to different ethnic groups, jealous of their cultural identity and traditions. There can be no question then in a country like Nigeria of one indigenous language being adopted as the single national language. So, while the various indigenous languages are employed in social and intimate contexts, for primary education and in some kinds of literature, English is used in public contexts, in secondary education and in literature which aims at a wide audience. English, the language of those Europeans who originally set the boundaries of the modern state, is now the essential agent of the state's cultural and political unity.

Clearly this necessary, almost enforced, retention of the former languages of subjection in African states must give rise to a certain frustration and hostility. The most intense example of this is of course to be found in the still subjected South Africa, where the Afrikaans language has become identified with oppression. Indeed the attempt to impose Afrikaans on black school-children as a means of instruction has led to riots.[2] Blacks passionately reject the language as the expression of a culture whose central values are racist. This situation is the product of South Africa's history, and no doubt there was a time when Afrikaans literature and Afrikaner culture could have adapted themselves to the coming post-colonial world. The coloured South African, Peter Abrahams, for instance, in his youth, even adopted Afrikaans as a literary medium, under the influence of a liberal Afrikaner teacher.

> In the end I forgot . . . his colour and we had long sessions on Afrikaans poetry and prose. Through him I discovered the rich body of Afrikaner literature and the beauty of the language itself. I wrote some Afrikaans verses which we discussed.[3]

Unfortunately Afrikanerdom has increasingly made such cultural flexibility impossible, and literature in Afrikaans has acted, according to Ezekiel Mphahlele (who was at school with Abrahams) as

> part of a defensive mechanism. The Afrikaners have put up barricades around themselves and the writer has to screw up his face and squint in order to see the outside landscape.[4]

The handful of non-whites who use Afrikaans as a means of literary expression isolate themselves from their own people. However, the close association of this language with white racism is not a sufficient reason in itself for its failure to find favour with non-whites. Far more important are its geographical limitations. As a specifically African version of Dutch it is not a language which gives the African, black, coloured or white, access to the wider world beyond his or her unjust society. In contrast the equally 'colonial' English is a world language, used not only in Britain and the United States, but also in many already independent non-white states throughout the world. English therefore, despite its colonial associations, is eagerly cultivated as a means of political and cultural self-assertion in the world at large.

The attitudes of South African non-whites towards the languages introduced by the whites illustrate in an extreme and unusually clear-cut form a pattern which recurs throughout Africa. Elsewhere English or French may be viewed as English is viewed in South Africa, as an instrument of education and advancement. Equally they may be viewed with an antagonism similar to that towards Afrikaans, as alien impositions. In West and Central Africa attitudes towards the colonial languages vary between the former French and the former British colonies. Attitudes towards French in former French territories tend to be the more extreme: either in acceptance or hostility. This is partly a result of the characteristic French emphasis on correctness and purity in language; but mostly of the French colonial policy of *assimilation*, under which indigenous cultures and languages were disregarded or suppressed, the aim being to educate the cleverest children to become black Frenchmen in every way. Ultimately it was envisaged that France and *France d'Outre-Mer* would become a political unity with no discrimination between its white and black citizens. This assimilation seems to have worked only too well, if with heavy ironies, in the case of the Camerounian, Mongo Beti, one of the most famous black writers in French. Although Beti's novels are caustic satires on the inhumanities and absurdities of colonialism, his narrators treat the traditional culture of their people with similar disrespect. In *Mission Terminée*[5] (1957) for instance, Beti's satire seems to cut both ways: against the French-educated protagonist and against the naive and uncouth villagers. The narrator views village life with a kind of farcical cynicism, not dissimilar to the indulgent contempt a cultivated Parisian might show towards the bumpkins of the French provinces. While the novel's occasional gestures

59

towards pastoral idyll are uneasily comic. The Guinean novelist, Camara Laye, presents a similarly complicated reaction to assimilation. On the one hand he shows a truly Gallic reverence for the French language; while on the other hand he asserts with religious fervour the values of Négritude and the 'African soul'.

> Through colonisation, French civilisation has taught us a language that we shall carefully preserve. But there is also much it has taken away from our own civilisation.
>
> Under the guidance of our President, His Excellency Sékou Touré, the first thing we did after independence, was to take hold of ourselves again. Very quickly, we picked up again our own music, our own literature, our own sculpture; all, that is to say, that was most deeply implanted in us and that had been slumbering during the sixty years of our colonisation. That is our new soul. [6]

Laye represents the religious, conservative African's reaction against assimilation by Europe. But at the same time, without feeling it to be a contradiction, he accepts the French language as something valuable, to be 'preserved'. Senghor, whose Négritude as we have already seen coexists with ardent Francophilia, shows a similar respect, terming French a language of 'graciousness and civility'.[7] And his expertise in French is such that he was among those called upon to perfect the language of the 1946 French constitution.

At the opposite extreme, Sembene Ousmane, the eminent Senegalese novelist and film-maker, expresses a lively antagonism towards the French language. Sembène, the political opposite of Senghor, began his writing career while he was leader of the Marseilles Dockers' Union, and later studied at the Moscow Film School. He naturally therefore, sees the language question in the political terms of class-conflict. He is acutely conscious of the cultural imperialism of the French language which aids and abets, in his eyes, the continued economic imperialism of France and her black agents in Senegal. So, although Sembène has no choice but to use French himself, or sacrifice his wider audience which is, as he says, 'in Europe', he insists (like Laye but for rather different reasons) that specifically African language and culture should be promoted in free African states.

> ... until we have made the African languages part of our educational system, in the primary schools and elsewhere, our literature will still be subject to the control of ther powers, or other people's good intentions. ... Dakar University ... is only a continuation of the French University. This does not seem to me to be a good thing. [8]

Although Sembène uses French in his novels, in his preferred medium of film he is able to embrace the opportunity offered by the serious cinema-goer's familiarity with subtitles to have his characters speak much of the time in Wolof, as they would in life. In his satirical film, *Xala*, the ideologies of the characters are often indicated by their choice of language. French is associated with corruption and insincerity, Wolof with honesty and genuine emotion. Just as the protagonist, a corrupt businessman, will drink only water imported in bottles from France, so also he speaks French at every opportunity in order to emphasize his social standing. His idealistic and radical daughter (who is a member of a Wolof society) insists on talking to him in Wolof even when he orders her to speak in French. At the climax of the action when the protagonist has gone bankrupt and his (equally corrupt) colleagues are formally expelling him from the 'Businessmen's Group' of the Senegalese Chamber of Commerce, he breaks through their hypocritical French in passionate Wolof, in order to express his contempt for the whole system. The committee at once erupts into a storm of Wolof abuse, until the President calls the meeting to order, exclaiming that even their insults should be in the 'purest tradition of Francophony'.[9]

In Anglophone Africa it is rare to find such ideologically clear-cut attitudes towards the colonial language, either of acceptance or rejection. This is partly because ideas about the purity and pre-eminence of English are not so zealously propagated as they are in the case of French. Also British colonial policy, as we have seen, was to save money by compromising with and adapting to indigenous culture, rather than attempting to extirpate it. Before independence the speaking of French was compulsory in the best French colonial schools, even at primary level. To speak one's native tongue, even in the playground, was to risk being stigmatised and humiliated, as is recorded in *Climbié* (1956), a novel by Bernard Dadié, the Minister of Culture of the Ivory Coast.[10] In the British colonies indigenous languages were employed in primary education, English becoming the exclusive language of instruction only at the secondary level. Anglophone Africans are consequently not usually so prickly and resentful about English, nor so devoted to it, as is frequently the case with French. The problem still remains however, with English as with French, that the language is an historical accident, imposed on Africa from outside and retained out of practical necessity. The use of English as a literary medium must involve conflicts and frustrations, especially in the years before and immediately following independence. The writer may even feel that in a real sense he or she *cannot* express African life in a European language. As Achebe has said in an oft-quoted remark:

> For an African, writing in English is not without its serious setbacks. He often finds himself describing situations or modes of thought which have no direct equivalent in the English way of life. [11]

Such reservations however do not prevent Achebe from writing in English. John Pepper Clark in a lively attack on a purist colleague who 'foresees a dead end to African Literature written in European languages', insists that such cultural translation *can* be made, although it is a subtle matter.

> In other words, the task for the Ijaw, and I dare say any Nigerian or African artist, writing in a European language like English, is one of finding the verbal equivalent for his characters created in their original and native context. The quest is not on the horizontal one of dialect and stress which are classifications of geography, society and education. It is on the vertical plane of what the schoolmasters call style and register, that is, the proper manner, level and range of dialogue and discussion.[12]

In the most successful cases, and he cites Achebe as one,

Clark considers that 'there is a faithful reproduction of the speech habits of one people into another language'.[13]

This discussion about whether English is suited in its grammar, syntax, idiom and register to express African 'modes of thought' is very much a cultural or aesthetic one. But an equally serious objection to English may be made on the less subtle level of practical politics. The writer may feel simply humiliated at having to use a 'colonial' language in a post-colonial world. More importantly indeed, the use of this European language cuts him off from the mass of his compatriots who lack Western education, not to mention those of his fellow Africans who use other European languages. The languages of Europe may thus appear as a political force, isolating the privileged elite from the mass of the people, and dividing African nations from each other. The poor communication between Anglophone and Francophone West Africa is notorious. It is as a result of such explicitly political dissatisfactions that the Kenyan, Ngugi wa Thiong'o, the Anglophone writer who is perhaps the most radical in his attitude towards language, has recently begun to turn to Kikuyu and to Swahili. Swahili is preferred as an 'African' language, having no origin in Europe; and, equally important, over much of East Africa it is the language spoken by the mass of the people. Ngugi's recent work written in Swahili has thus reached much wider audiences within East Africa, than his works in English.[14] Swahili possesses certain unique advantages among African languages. It is not associated with any particular ethnic group, nor even with any particular nation, being widespread in Somalia, Uganda, Tanzania and Kenya. Consequently, it is the ideal language for a politically radical writer like Ngugi, who wishes to reach the lowest social classes without resorting to a narrow, ethnically divisive means of expression.

Unfortunately these advantages are not shared by any language elsewhere in Africa. In West Africa for instance the writer must use either the widespread but elitist English or French, or a more or less ethnically exclusive indigenous language. Politically conscious Africans have long been impatient of the restrictions to which this situation condemns them. The possibility of a non-European *lingua franca* has been discussed since the early days of pan-Africanism. One of the resolutions passed at the (mainly Francophone) Second Conference of Negro Writers and Artists which took place in Rome in 1958 called for one language to be chosen, on merit, and improved by a sort of *Académie Africaine.*

ii) . . . one African language should be chosen. This would not necessarily belong to a relative majority of peoples since the richness and character of a language are more important qualities linguistically. All Africans would learn this national language besides their own regional language and the European language of secondary education (English, French, etc.); the latter would be optional.

iii) a team of linguists would be instructed to enrich this language, as rapidly as possible, with the terminology necessary for the expression of modern philosophy, science and technology. [15]

This idealistic proposal has so far, not surprisingly perhaps, come to nothing. The most practicable candidate for the status of *lingua franca* remains Swahili, which as we have seen already possesses a certain supra-national position. Wole Soyinka envisages Swahili becoming *the* African second language. All significant writing by Africans would be translated into Swahili, whether written originally in European or indigenous languages. The Swahili versions would not supersede the originals, but would ensure that all African writing was accessible to all Africans, whatever their traditional or colonial background. Swahili would also be spoken between Africans without other shared languages. It would thus perform something of the continental unifying function that the pan-European Latin performed during the Middle Ages: although it would not, it is hoped, remain the property of an exclusive elite, as Latin was. The advantages of Soyinka's proposals are obvious. But the difficulties and objections to them are equally obvious, particularly in the case of countries such as Soyinka's own Nigeria where Swahili is not already established. In the first place those parts of Africa where Swahili is at present used would gain a definite advantage, politically and culturally, over those parts where it is not. Moreover everywhere except East Africa it would remain for the foreseeable future very much a second language. The use of Swahili by a Nigerian or in translating Nigerian literature, will for example solve none of the problems referred to by Achebe and Clark. 'African' though it may be, it is very doubtful whether Swahili is any better suited than, say, English, to express the modes of thought and nuances of feeling of people whose native tongue is Hausa, Ijaw or Tiv. But most important of all, the massive educational programme that would be needed to spread Swahili throughout Africa, will not be forthcoming. There is neither the political will for such an effort, nor the human and technical resources, in a continent where basic literacy is still the most urgent educational concern.

In Nigeria, as in most of Africa then the choice for the writer is between his vernacular and his European second language. The use of either imposes limitations on expression and audience unknown to the fortunate British writer in his virtually monolingual culture. The use of an indigenous language allows full expression of the writer's Africanness, but reduces his audience, sometimes drastically. It also involves the problems attendant on a literature in the process of emerging from the oral phase: the adaptation of traditional forms and the development of new, even the devising or perfecting of an orthography. The use of English involves adaptation to a second language, but gives access to the widest audience both inside Africa (among the more highly educated only) and outside. The third possibility which should be mentioned, pidgin, a *lingua franca* in much of coastal West Africa, has found no favour among serious writers. As a simplified variant of English evolved to facilitate communication between colonial master and servant it promises little as a literary medium. Nor does it seem likely to develop in Africa, as it has in Papua New Guinea and the Solomon Islands, the necessary richness and complexity. It has up to now been used not as a primary literary medium, but for characterisation and authentic 'colour' in novels in English, and often in comic contexts.

In Nigeria it is government policy to encourage the wider use of indigenous languages. In the words of the 1977 White Paper, 'National Policy in Education':

> In addition to appreciating the importance of language in the educational process, and as a means of preserving the people's culture, the Government considers it to be in the interest of national unity that each child should be encouraged to learn one of the three major languages other than his own mother-tongue. In this connection, the Government considers the three major languages in Nigeria to be Hausa, Ibo and Yoruba.[16]

If this aim can eventually be made a reality then literature in these three languages may become in a real sense *Nigerian* literature. An anthology of criticism which treats literature in indigenous languages alongside that in English has recently been published, entitled *Critical Perspectives on Nigerian Literatures*,[17] the plural being highly significant. As yet, since there is no such language as Nigerian, 'Nigerian literature' must mean that written in the only language in regular use throughout the Federation—English. How then have Nigerian writers come to terms with the various problems involved in the use of this second language? The kinds of English they use differ greatly one from another, some showing the boldest modifications of grammar and syntax, while others appear at first sight little different from conventional English. Some writers (more or less consciously) subvert and refashion English in the attempt to express themselves authentically. Others use English with the unforced fluency one might expect of someone writing in his first language.

## Amos Tutuola: 'The Palm-Wine Drinkard' (1952)

Amos Tutuola, the earliest Nigerian writer of fiction to achieve publication presents us with one of the most radical refashionings of English in Nigerian literature. He is of particular interest since, ironically, those early critics loudest in praise of his 'Africanness' and most admiring of his stylistic distortions were English or American; whereas his fellow Nigerians are often embarrassed by his 'bad' English. Tutuola is by European criteria an unusual man to have become a famous author. He began his formal education at the age of fourteen and it was broken off when he was nineteen, in 1939. After trying farming without success, he trained in smithery, and in 1942 he joined the RAF as a blacksmith. It was after the war that he embarked on his writing career.

> I got employment in the Department of Labour, Lagos, in 1946, as a messenger. I was still in this hardship and poverty, when one night, it came to my mind to write my first book—*The Palm-Wine Drinkard* and I wrote it within a few days successfully because I was a story-teller when I was at school. So since then I have become a writer.[18]

The manuscript found its way, *via* The United Society for Christian Literature, to Faber and Faber in London, who published it in 1952.

*The Palm-Wine Drinkard* is a naive romance, a sequence of folk-tales loosely unified by the first-person narrator who is journeying to 'Deads' Town' in quest of his palm-wine tapster, who has fallen from a tree and been killed. The story is told in misspelled English with unorthodox grammar and syntax. Its narrative coherence is similarly loose. A short episode will illustrate its qualities. The narrator has been sent by an old man to capture Death in a net. He reaches Death's home.

> Nobody was living near or with him there, he was living lonely, even bush animals and birds were very far away from his house. So when I wanted to sleep at night, he gave me a wide black cover cloth and then gave me a separate room to sleep inside, but when I entered the room, I met a bed which was made with bones of human-beings; but as this bed was terrible to look at or to sleep on it, I slept under it instead, because I knew his trick already. Even as this bed was very terrible, I was unable to sleep under as I lied down there because of fear of the bones of human-beings, but I lied down there awoke. To my surprise was that when it was about two o'clock in the midnight, there I saw somebody enter into the room cautiously with a heavy club in his hands, he came nearer to the bed on which he had told me to sleep, then he clubbed the bed with all his power . . . [19]

The narrative logic is faulty. The narrator lies under the bed 'because I knew his trick already', yet 'To my surprise was' that Death clubs the bed. The grammatical and spelling mistakes are of an elementary kind: 'a separate room to sleep inside', 'lied', 'awoke'. The syntax is also elementary, long sequences of clauses being divided only by commas, or linked by 'and', 'but', 'then' or 'so'. The overall narrative at this point also lacks coherence. When the narrator finally captures Death in his net, he brings him back to the old man's town and despite the protests of the inhabitants, throws him down, upon which the net splits and Death breaks free.

> So that since the day that I had brought Death out from his house, he has no permanent place to dwell or stay, and we are hearing his name about in the world. [20]

But if Death was not 'about in the world' before this episode, how does the narrator come to be on a quest for his dead tapster? Similar self-contradictions abound in the book. At times the narrator, whose name is 'Father of gods who could do anything in this world' is a kind of all-powerful 'god and a ju-ju man'. At various times he changes himself into a bird, a lizard and even a ferry-boat, the fare for which is 3d., collected by his wife. Another time he dissolves into air. At other times again, however, he is quite powerless against the wraiths and monsters which attack him. Now and then he explains that this is because his ju-ju is weak from overuse, but sometimes he gives no reason for his powerlessness. Obviously the author has not cared to ensure that the different folk-tales he has used are consistent with each other.

The language which Tutuola uses has been analysed by a fellow Yoruba, A. Afolayan, in an essay published in Christopher Heywood's *Perspectives on African Literature*. Afolayan's verdict is that Tutuola is writing in his second language using the grammar and idioms of his first, the result being 'Yoruba English'.

> . . . his English is that of the Yoruba user, not of the average educated user but of generally the user with post-primary education at approximately the level of present-day Secondary Class Four. [21]

Tutuola is organising his Yoruba material in the Yoruba language and then writing it down direct in English, in a process involving 'some sort of translation'.[22] 'I met a bed' for instance is, as Afolayan tells us, a literal translation of the idiomatic Yoruba phrase. One of Tutuola's most persistent traits is his avoidance of pronouns, the noun itself being repeated; or alternatively the insertion of the relevant noun in brackets after the pronoun. This makes his style oddly repetitive.

> This was how I brought out Death to the old man who told me to go and bring him before he (old man) would tell me whereabouts my palm-wine tapster was that I was looking for before I reached that town and went to the old man. [23]

As Afolayan tells us this feature is partly the result of the fact that there is only one form of the third person singular pronoun in Yoruba: 'o', which stands equally for 'he', 'she' or 'it'. Repetition of nouns where in English pronouns would be used, is thus common in Yoruba, even when not strictly required in the interests of clarity. At other times Tutuola simply translates characteristic Yoruba clause-structures into English: for example 'We reached a river which crossed our way to pass'. Other features, such as weak past tenses for strong verbs ('lied') and unusual tense constructions ('was sat down') are the common mistakes of anyone in the process of learning English, whether a non-English speaker or an English child.

Afolayan's analysis might lead one to find little remarkable in Tutuola's language, typical as it is of Yoruba English. Afolayan quotes from essays by Yoruba schoolchildren which show exactly the same features. If Tutuola's is a radical refashioning of English it is an ingenuous, even unconscious one, lively in its way but with the same lack of purposiveness as is revealed in the structure of the narrative. The interest of Tutuola's case from our point of view lies in the reactions of his earliest critics who were at that time of course, all Europeans or Americans. The first critical response to *The Palm-Wine Drinkard* came in a review in *The Observer* by

Dylan Thomas. Thomas was enthusiastic. 'Nothing is too prodigious or too trivial to put down in this tall, devilish story', [24] he wrote, and added that it was in 'young English by a West African'. One might suspect here that 'young' is a polite synonym for 'childlike' from a poet who revelled in the childlike. However, later more academic critics followed Thomas's lead by analysing the 'new' African quality in Tutuola's language and narrative techniques. Charles R. Larson for instance in his book *The Emergence of African Fiction* devotes a chapter to the authentic 'Africanness' of Tutuola's vision, entitled grandly: 'Time, Space and Description: The Tutuolan World'. He argues that Tutuola, as an African, is living in a world radically different, spatially, temporally and even physically, from that of a European. This is why his language lacks the structures of normal English and why his narrative is apparently inconsequential and self-contradictory. The 'European' notions of cause and effect and of natural scientific laws are as irrelevant to Tutuola's work as the rules of English grammar. Larson quotes the Canadian critic, Margaret Laurence, on the profoundly symbolic, inner quality of Tutuola's reality.

> Tutuola writes best when most intuitively and most intensely inward. His forests are certainly and in detail the outer ones[25] but they are, as well, the forests of the mind, where the individual meets and grapples with the creatures of his own imagination. These creatures are aspects of himself, aspects of his response to the world into which he was born, the world to which he must continue to return if he is to live as a man. [26]

Larson's and Laurence's analyses are all very portentous and impressive. But what are they saying? They seem to imply that by ignoring the coherences of grammar and of plausibility and cause and effect, Tutuola has put himself on the same level of post-Freudian symbolic profundity as an early twentieth-century European modernist: that Tutuola's style is inventive in the same way as that of the modernists, and that he is concerned in the same way with conscious and subconscious, symbol and archetype. Margaret Laurence's critical language is no different from that one might use of Proust or D.H. Lawrence. Larson indeed even goes so far as to annex Tutuola to a specific modernist movement, calling him a 'surrealist', but then making the odd qualification:

> This surrealism is indigenous or even spontaneous, not based on Tutuola's knowledge of the French surrealist movement. [27]

It is difficult to see what the word 'surrealist' can mean in this context. In France *surréalisme* was a reaction against the entrenched respectability of *réalisme*, an attempt to rise 'above' it. Larson is clearly right to dissociate Tutuola from this, since Tutuola has no Nigerian realism to transcend and clearly has little notion of European realism. So in what sense can he possibly be called 'surrealist'? Margaret Laurence and Larson have allowed their literary critical categories to lead them astray. *The Palm-Wine Drinkard* possesses mythical elements, as do all folk-tales. The story of the capture and release of Death resembles the Greek myth of Pandora's box for instance. But this is a far cry from the 'forests of the mind' and the surrealism of twentieth-century Europe. If *The Palm-Wine Drinkard* is surrealist it is so in the same sense that *Hansel and Gretel* and *Jack and the Beanstalk* are surrealist.

At the bottom of Larson's version of Tutuola lies a peculiarly complex variation of cultural imperialism, one which is found in different forms in other non-African critics of African writing (and indeed in some African critics). The Western reader's initial reaction to Tutuola's Yoruba English will probably be to find it quaint; and Larson is unwilling to find Tutuola quaint in case he should be convicted of the crudest kind of cultural imperialism—indulgent condescension. On the other hand Larson is also determined, as was Rousseau before him, to find in this distant culture something radically different from that of the West, and something that will teach the West a lesson. The result is that he finds philosophical profundity and surrealism in Tutuola's Secondary Class Four English version of Yoruba folk-tales. The early history of West African fiction has been marked by many such examples of Western critics *using* Africa for their own cultural purposes.

Ayi Kwei Armah has suggested the term 'Larsony' for such distortion,[28] while Wole Soyinka has imaged it in terms of the old colonialism. At the first sign, he relates, a flock of vulture-like Western publishers and literary men descended upon Africa eager to tear bits off the 'stillborn foetus of the African Muse'. [29] The West's material plundering of Africa is now matched by a cultural plundering, conducted with the same well-organised rapacity. Whatever Africa has produced by way of literature has been seized on by European and American critics and academics in search of new fields into which to expand, new academic empires to build. As an American 'Africanist' remarks in one of Armah's novels: 'Africa is now an area justifying advanced study, you know'.[30] Soyinka, perhaps with some exaggeration, declares: 'the average published writer in the first few years of the post-colonial era was the most celebrated skin of inconsequence to cover the true flesh of the African dilemma'.[31] It is instructive then to compare the American, Larson's rich and complex web of academic critical vocabulary with the Nigerian, Afolayan's businesslike and practical analysis. Without Larson's need to avoid the accusation of Western condescension Afolayan is at liberty to find Tutuola's English 'incorrect'; and being Nigerian, he does not feel it necessary to devote much energy to proving that incoherence and self-contradiction are profoundly African qualities. Far from being the masterful misuse of English which some critics imply, Tutuola's unorthodox English is, as Afolayan shows, inadvertent. 'One may even suggest that Tutuola thinks that he is correct when he writes.' [32]

Achebe has drawn attention to the dangers of distorting English too freely.

> It can lead to *bad* English being accepted and defended as African or Nigerian. I submit that those who can do the work of extending the frontiers of English so as to accommodate African thought-patterns must do it through their mastery of English and not out of innocence.[33]

He allows Tutuola a genuine vitality, but insists 'it is possible that he has done something unique and interesting in a way that is not susceptible to further development'.[34] Like the medieval romance, *Ywain and Gawain*, or like Malory's Arthurian tales, which use similarly simple syntax and show similar incoherences of narrative, *The Palm-Wine Drinkard* will retain an historical significance, and a certain real if limited literary value. Tutuola's own sensible and unpretentious, if somewhat innocent, assessment of his own work given in an interview in the Nigerian *Sunday Times*, may speak for itself.

| | |
|---|---|
| SUNDAY TIMES: | How many foreign languages are your works now being printed [in?] |
| TUTUOLA: | Over 10. |
| SUNDAY TIMES: | Do you think this is because they think your work is regarded as illiterate and the type that should come from Africa? |
| TUTUOLA: | Local publishers want classroom textbooks from writers, they want polished English. Those people are much more interested in content and style. |
| SUNDAY TIMES: | Are you aware that your work is being used as recommended texts in some universities? |
| TUTUOLA: | No[.] I am not aware. |
| SUNDAY TIMES: | What is your literary antecedent? |
| TUTUOLA: | We always tell stories at school and in my village. I don't forge stories. I only reproduce them. There was a lady at school who I always wanted to beat because she was a fantastic story-teiler.[35] |

## Gabriel Okara: 'The Voice' (1964)

Tutuola is not the only Nigerian writer to meet the problem of expressing African life in English language by boldly 'translating' from his native tongue. Gabriel Okara presents an interesting contrast with Tutuola and brings up, perhaps in a more significant form, the question of the relation of West African English to English English. Okara is, unlike Tutuola, quite self-conscious and deliberate in his technique.

73

As a writer who believes in the utilisation of African ideas, African philosophy and African folk-lore and imagery to the fullest extent possible, I am of the opinion the only way to use them effectively is to translate them almost literally from the African language native to the writer into whatever European language he is using as his medium of expression. [36]

As he says he found it difficult at first to stop himself expressing his ideas first in English. Each Ijaw expression needed careful analysis to discover the nearest equivalent in English. But by this means Okara hopes to rescue his native Ijaw culture from the stifling embrace of the English culture and language which threaten it.

The results of Okara's methods in his short novel, *The Voice*, are startling and successful. Often an Ijaw idiom can strike the English or American reader with extraordinary freshness.

They ran with the backs of their feet touching the backs of their heads. Who would want to die of itches? No one. So they ran with all their insides and with all their shadows. [37]

No reader can mistake the meaning of 'insides' and 'shadows' here, although there is no idiomatic equivalent in orthodox English (perhaps 'guts' is an approximate parallel). These words expand the metaphorical range of English with little feeling of strain. Similarly, the distortions of syntax never make the meaning obscure. Usually they reinforce it. When Okolo, a man of passionate integrity, is wrongly accused of a crime, his negatives jut out of the sentences at all angles.

'You cannot a thing I have done not put on my head.' Thus strongly Okolo spoke. 'How can you on my head put a thing that happened not? It is true I have spoken not to anyone since the canoe I entered. That was because my inside is filled with forcing thoughts up to my throat which I dare speak not.' [38]

The contortions here, though violent, are not unprecedented, even in works by Britons. One may be reminded in reading *The Voice* of Dylan Thomas, Gerard Manley Hopkins, even of Milton. Okara then modifies his English with a sense of its inherent, traditional qualities; and most important, his modifications always have some meaningful literary point. There is an artistic discipline at work. The discipline is so thorough and coherent that at one point Okara can go so far as to introduce a 'foreign' English proverb, translated into his Ijaw English.

'I am—I mean—we are soft-hearted people, soft like water,' Izongo said, raising his eyes to the eye of the sky as if trying to see the root of nature's wonders. 'Our insides are soft like water even if you say our insides are filled with stone. Our eyes too are soft and they cannot fall on suffering. We have been turning it even in our insides since you threw your back at us and left. Our highest son, Abadi, has been telling me an English saying, which I agree fits you, and that saying is that when I do not see you, you will not be in my inside.'[39]

In the midst of Okara's Ijaw idioms the formulation 'Out of sight, out of mind' would inevitably appear as a foreign language. So it must be 'translated' into the correct Ijaw form.

Okara's case, like that of Tutuola, brings up the question of how far this refashioning of English can go before it becomes, in effect, a new language, requiring a new and unprecedented response from the reader and a new approach from the literary critic. To put it more crudely, are such African versions of English abandoning the wider audience outside Africa? Afolayan goes so far as to suggest that possibly only native Yoruba-speakers can fully enjoy or appreciate Tutuola's work, because only they speak its language. By the same token one could argue that only native Ijaw-speakers can fully appreciate Okara. Even further, it has been argued that even in apparently 'correct' English used by West Africans, the essential African nuances and inflections will not be fully understood by the European or American reader. Even the moderate Chinua Achebe has on occasions taken this culturally absolutist position.

No man can understand another whose language he does not speak (and 'language' here does not mean simply words, but a man's entire world view). How many Europeans and Americans have our language? I do not know of any, certainly not among our writers and critics.[40]

75

There is a certain ambiguity here, and Achebe *could* be taken to imply that one can understand a man's 'world view' without necessarily understanding his 'words'. This is not what he says however, and he seems to want to insist that language in the literal sense is the key to, though not a guarantee of, any wider cultural understanding. Are we to accept this extreme position on the cultural centrality of language, in all its implications? Does Achebe feel that no Ibo writer, such as himself, who does not know (say) Ijaw, or Edo or Fulfulde or any of the other languages of Nigeria, should ever include a man or woman from such a language group in a novel, because he cannot 'understand' them? Can an Englishman not 'understand' Solzhenitsyn because he has no Russian, and reads him in translation? Surely this is to make language into a mystique: a barrier between people, rather than a means of communication between them. There can be no doubt that language enshrines cultural values. But are the differences between cultures so great or the subtler distinctions between them of such central importance that no translation is possible without total distortion?

Common sense tells us that language is a flexible and robust thing. Despite all his innovations Okara is, after all, still writing in English, and what is more, in an effective English which conveys the essential meaning of his work to any English-speaker. Indeed, for the vast majority of readers the fact that Okara's stylistic effects are the result of a translation from Ijaw, and reflect Ijaw culture, is of no essential significance. The style is coherent simply as an English style and so dictates its own appropriate and distinctive response. To such readers as will never visit the Ijaw-speaking region of Nigeria, nor ever meet an Ijaw-speaker, the fact that the modifications of English are an attempt to recreate Ijaw modes of thought is of the same significance as the fact that Swift was expressing characteristically early eighteenth century modes of thought. It is of interest certainly, and demanding of further investigation by the specialist; but it is by no means a crucial element in any appreciation of Swift's works as literature. This is the more easy to see in the case of

Okara since his theme is unmistakably a universal one. *The Voice* is a political fable, similar to those of Kafka, by whom Okara has been influenced. Okolo (whose name in Ijaw means 'voice') is searching for 'It'. 'It' is never defined. Okolo even says that 'It' may be different for different people. 'It' is clearly a symbol for a certain kind of personal integrity. The search for 'It' keeps a man's or a woman's 'insides' 'straight' or 'sweet'. The powers that be, the corrupt village chief, Izongo, and his henchmen, pursue Okolo for thus daring to think for himself. They exile him, and finally, when he returns, they murder him. The African village, with its elders, its small population and sense of community, its easily aroused superstition against 'witches', becomes a suitable microcosm in which to expound this universal message. It is also con-cretely and convincingly African.

## Chinua Achebe: 'Things Fall Apart' (1958)

Okara then succeeds because, for all his boldness of technique, he writes with a genuine feeling for the potential of English. He thus illustrates the method of approach which Achebe feels most appropriate to the assertion of an African cultural identity. The Nigerian, Achebe insists, must first master English, before modifying it. 'It is important first to learn the rules of English and afterwards break them if we wish.'[41] It is only through such a compromise with the second language that the African writer can assert his culture in the wider world.

> The African writer should aim to use English in a way that brings out his message best without altering the language to the extent that its value as a medium of international exchange will be lost. He should aim at fashioning out an English which is at once universal and able to carry his peculiar experience.[42]

Okara's is a particularly bold and adventurous form of this compromise. Achebe's own appears at first sight far less radical. The English he uses in his first novel about traditional

77

Ibo life, *Things Fall Apart*, seems beguilingly bland and correct.

> He was tall and huge, and his bushy eyebrows and wide nose gave him a very severe look. He breathed heavily, and it was said that, when he slept, his wives and children in their out-houses could hear him breathe. When he walked, his heels hardly touched the ground and he seemed to walk on springs, as if he was going to pounce on somebody. And he did pounce on people quite often. He had a slight stammer and whenever he was angry and could not get his words out quickly enough, he would use his fists. He had no patience with unsuccessful men. He had no patience with his father.[43]

Even when the emotions involved are intense and complex the language remains relatively colourless. This is the case when Okonkwo, out of a stubborn fear of being thought weak, takes part in the ritual murder of Ikemefuna, the boy hostage who has become his beloved foster-son.

> As the man who had cleared his throat drew up and raised his matchet, Okonkwo looked away. He heard the blow. The pot fell and broke in the sand. He heard Ikemefuna cry, 'My father, they have killed me!' as he ran towards him. Dazed with fear, Okonkwo drew his matchet and cut him down. He was afraid of being thought weak.[44]

At this point there is an emotional impact in the very starkness and undemonstrativeness of the language ('The pot fell and broke in the sand.') But its unemphatic quality throughout the novel may strike the English or American reader, on first reading, as strange. The narrative's distinctive colour comes from the frequent Ibo proverbs which construct the complex picture of Ibo tradition and philosophy for which the novel is famous.[45] Otherwise it is very cool.

There are several reasons for this, not least Achebe's individual personality. 'Restraint' he has said, 'well that's my style, you see.'[46] But an important reason also must lie in the very nature of English as used in Nigeria. To the majority of Nigerians English is a scarcely known or little used second language. And even for most educated people, in the bureaucracy and the universities, English is rather the language of formal communication—in teaching, for use with expatriates or people from different ethnic groups—than the usual language of social life or intimacy. The result of this is that, although English is constantly developing new, Nigerian distinctions of register among groups where it is in regular use, a distinct kind of English has developed for communication of the widest kind, which lacks nuances of class and social register. This level of language is to a great extent insulated from the class and ethnic differences within Nigeria—hence its political usefulness. But hence also what has been called its 'cleanness'. Much 'correct' Nigerian English is 'clean', without the different registers and social implications which develop with constant promiscuous use. Peter Young has discussed the dreary informational tone of much West African writing in English, associating it with the intense pressure on the young to succeed in formal examinations.

> The pressures upon a student in West Africa to succeed are enormous and more responsibility falls upon him than is generally felt by his European counterpart. Consequently, he spends a great deal of time on books required for examinations. He is bound by highly formal requirements and reading for pleasure is for most a luxury. His linguistic limitations bind him to an environment of textbook language, and it is hardly surprising that for him this is often the most normal type of English. [47]

Achebe himself has drawn attention to the 'competent', un-inspired work of writers who use this strangely detached kind of English without sensitivity.[48] In his case however the 'cleanness' of the language of his two village novels is not merely uninspired. It has indeed been put to subtle and ingenious use.

Achebe sees his purpose in this novel as twofold. Firstly it is an attempt, like Okara's, at 'cultural retrieval', aimed at rescuing his traditional culture from the myths and distortions of the colonialist. He would be content he says, in a famous remark, if this novel does

> no more than teach my readers that their past—with all its imperfections—was not one long night of savagery from which the first Europeans acting on God's behalf delivered them. [49]

79

This is the African writer's primary political commitment. On the other hand he is aware of the equally dangerous myths and distortions which such a commitment may entail. The qualification, 'with all its imperfections', is a characteristic one. It is equally part of his purpose to avoid irresponsible idealisation. We have already seen his insistance that the past was not 'one long, technicolour idyll'. Achebe then must steer a stylistic middle course between the Scylla of Conrad and Ryder Haggard, towards which the traditions of the English language drive him; and the Charybdis of idealisation, which does perhaps threaten the work of other Nigerian writers such as Elechi Amadi and Flora Nwapa—although, in the case of Nwapa particularly, the language is so 'clean' that the term 'technicolour' is not appropriate. It is here that Achebe's skill in handling 'clean' English, and his stylistic restraint stand him in good stead. In the first place, as a medium for conveying the life of an untouched village, lacking the social and individual diversity which come with development, this 'clean' English is ideal. Moreover its unforced but unmistakable difference from normal literary English keeps the reader constantly aware that the villagers are throughout to be understood as speaking not in English but in Ibo. Furthermore, as David Carroll has shown[50] this undemonstrative, matter-of-fact English is the perfect antidote to the melodrama of the European 'dark continent' view of Africa. Where Conrad's Marlow in *Heart of Darkness* (1902), misled by external appearances, sees a 'terrible frankness',[51] a primeval chaos in the native dances which he witnesses, Achebe reveals an orderly, even ordinary, social life, with a quiet formality of manners.

> 'I do not know how to thank you.'
> 'I can tell you,' said Obierika. 'Kill one of your sons for me.'
> 'That will not be enough,' said Okonkwo.
> 'Then kill yourself,' said Obierika.
> 'Forgive me,' said Okonkwo, smiling. 'I shall not talk about thanking you any more.' [52]

At the same time however this even-paced narrative medium can, as we have seen, relate the less acceptable aspects of traditional custom which are generally omitted from or subtly excused in the works of Amadi and Nwapa, without introducing the lurid emotionalism of Conrad's and other European views of Africa. The style possesses a dispassionateness which neither condemns nor attempts to excuse.

Achebe's apparently colourless English then reveals itself on analysis to be part of a subtle rhetorical strategy. Subtler indeed than that urged on the post-colonial writer by Jean-Paul Sartre.

> Since the oppressor is present even in the language that they speak, they will use that language to destroy him ... The black herald will strip from words their Frenchness, will shatter them, will destroy their traditional associations and will juxtapose them with violence.[53]

What Achebe has done in *Things Fall Apart* bears some relation to what Sartre is describing, and perhaps there is a place for a more violently kathartic approach to language. But Sartre's heady and emotional tone looks suspiciously like a later version of Conrad's: betraying another, rather different, attempt to use Africa as a tool in the working out of essentially European frustrations and boredoms. The destruction Sartre envisages may seem to many Africans a cultural luxury, which only Europe and the United States can afford. So, paradoxically, Achebe's apparently simple, 'correct' English may be a more authentic voice of Africa here; the more effective method of cultural decolonisation, for both his African and white readers. It meets the colonial myths on their own linguistic ground, and is in its way far more persuasive than on the one hand an 'attack' on the colonial language, or on the other an uncritical nostalgia for pre-colonial traditions such as one finds in some Nigerian novels.

# 3 Democracy and the elite: T.M. Aluko

## One Man, One Matchet (1964)

Timothy Mofolorunso Aluko is one of the oldest Nigerian writers, having been born in 1918, although his first novel, *One Man, One Wife*, did not appear until 1959, the year after the much younger Achebe's *Things Fall Apart*. His seniority means that his formative years were spent securely in the colonial period, which helps to account for the tinny and hollow 'progressiveness' of tone which places him firmly in the first phase of colonial and post-colonial literature as described by Fanon. In this phase, Fanon says, we find an 'unqualified assimilation' of the coloniser's attitudes and literary styles.

> In the first phase, the native intellectual gives proof that he has assimilated the culture of the occupying power. His writings correspond point by point with those of his opposite numbers in the mother country ... This is the period of unqualified assimilation.[1]

As Fanon's analysis of this phase leads us to expect, Aluko's novels echo British models; although British literary movements being less programmatic than French, stylistic parallels are not as close as they are in the case of some French writers. Aluko's work belongs to the minor tradition of H.G. Wells's social-problem novels—what Wells himself termed 'discussion novels'—with their sketchy, conventionally realistic characterisation, mechanical plots, and explicit discussions of topical issues. In Britain C.P. Snow is the most notable writer to continue this tradition, and his work shows some broad similarities to Aluko's. Like Wells and Snow Aluko was not trained in the arts. His education was in civil engineering and town-planning, at Yaba College and in London. In 1956 he was appointed Town Engineer to the Lagos Town Council, and in 1960, on Independence, became Director of Public Works for Western Nigeria. It was while holding this top administrative post that he wrote his most successful novel, *One Man, One Matchet*. His views on politics are thus not simply those of a novelist, but also those of a high-ranking civil servant.

In *One Man, One Matchet* Aluko shows himself to possess the enlightened, progressive yet practical attitudes which the more thoughtful colonial administrators wished to instil into their black successors. Indeed the novel, set in 1949, concerns the handing on of authority by a white colonial administrator, Stanfield, favourably portrayed by Aluko, to a black successor. It is significant that it should be William Walsh, author of *Commonwealth Literature* and a very orthodox, English sort of commentator who gives the most favourable critical attention to Aluko's work, referring to his 'masculine energy', his 'solid and shapely novels' (a judgement which few other critics would accept), and praising his lack of 'arrogance or fanaticism'.[2] To the Ugandan critic, Shatto Arthur Gakwandi, whose perspective is more alive to ideological issues, the qualities which impress Walsh with Aluko's moderation and common sense, are sure signs that he is still enslaved to the world-view of his former British masters.

> Aluko's politics are reactionary and authoritarian. He advocates some kind of dictatorship by the highly educated Africans. He hardly concerns himself with ideas and policies: his pre-occupation is with civil service regulations and procedures. He writes as a member of the establishment and suggests no radical transformation of this colonial establishment. All he wishes to see is a few men of integrity stepping into the shoes of the colonial administrators.[3]

This view of Aluko gains ample confirmation from the most overtly political sections of *One Man, One Matchet*. In the closing pages Aluko takes the opportunity, now that the action of the novel has been disposed of, to canvas a variety of issues which he considers of public concern. His protagonist, Udo Akpan, who acts as his mouthpiece here, runs through a strangely miscellaneous list of grievances. He laments the influence of tribalism. He questions whether the British legal practice of assuming innocence until proof of guilt is established does not encourage crime in volatile and unruly Nigeria. He attacks the time-consuming practice of conducting postmortems on the victims of every fatal accident. He advocates allowing civil servants to play an active part in politics, since there are so few educated men in Nigeria that society cannot afford to lose their political talents by compelling their impartiality. He deplores the drain on public expenditure caused by the lavish entertainment expenses required for traditional hospitality. And so on. The common factor in every case is a call for the cutting of legal or administrative corners in order to ensure greater efficiency by affording greater powers of discretion to the public servant. No one who has any knowledge of Nigeria can deny that greater administrative efficiency is urgently needed; but the particular reforms Akpan proposes are questionable. Does Aluko seriously advocate a judicial system for Nigeria in which the guilt of the accused can be assumed simply on the word of someone in authority? Does he really consider it desirable for civil servants to be publicly committed to party-politics, with all the conflicts of loyalty which would be bound to ensue? The inevitable consequences of such measures, in abuses and corruption, must be obvious to all but the most politically naive. Aluko is clearly speaking here on behalf of a sectional interest, the interest of the civil servant, impatient of the political and legal restraints on what he conceives to be the efficient execution of his duties. He shows no insight into the implications of his suggestions for society as a whole.

Nevertheless Aluko's analyses of political issues cannot simply be dismissed. However biased and inadequate his practical suggestions may be they are a natural and understandable response to the Nigerian situation as he portrays it. His diagnosis is undeniably correct in essence; it is the prognosis which is questionable. His depiction of political realities 'on the ground' often possesses a realism, an urgency and conviction which bears ample witness to his practical experience in local government. His analyses indeed possess a clarity and precision verging on the diagrammatic. Early in *One Man, One Matchet* Akpan, the aspiring new black District Officer, makes a stirring and lucid speech to the inhabitants of the Yoruba village of Ipaja about the necessity of paying their taxes.

'You cannot ask for progress and independence with one voice and at the same time refuse to accept the responsibilities that come with progress and independence.[4]

He goes on to explain that the taxes are needed to pay for the pure water-supply for which the villagers are all clamouring. This is, one might have thought, simple common sense. And Akpan flatters himself on the clarity with which he has put over his point. However, his words are thrown away on the villagers, who are too preoccupied with the fact that he comes from a different tribe (his name suggests that he is from the South-east of Nigeria) to consider what he has actually said. The fact that he has addressed them in English is, significantly, the conclusive point as far as they are concerned.

'He is not one of our own tribe,' another observed regretfully. 'We do not understand his language. He does not understand ours. How then can he see things like us?'[5]

The result is that the people stubbornly withhold their taxes and the water-supply remains unsatisfactory. Aluko's moral is clear. The democratic system bequeathed to Nigeria by Britain, which he himself admires, can only work with the co-operation and consent of the people: but this consent is very difficult to obtain from a population whose horizons are entirely tribal and local, and who lack any conception of the political system.

Aluko's portrayal of the villagers of Ipaja shows a lively grasp of communal psychology and a talent for neat and telling caricature. The villagers show all the selfish short-sightedness of children, and something also of the child's exasperating innocence. Indeed if Aluko were white he would certainly be accused of a patronising and racist condescension towards them! Chief Momo's speech on the taxation issue which follows Akpan's (but which, being in Yoruba Akpan

85

cannot understand) illustrates this.

'Who in Ipaja does not know that the first assessment is always too high? When the Clerk first writes down three pounds for you, do you not go to beg the Chiefs and do you not go to see the Clerk at home? When you do this, do they not have mercy on you and do they not ask you to pay fifteen shillings instead of the original three pounds? And after paying the Kola for the Oba and Chiefs and the Clerk, you still pay less than the original three pounds which the Clerk first writes against your name. And everyone is happy—you, the Oba and Chiefs—and is the Clerk not happy?' and he looked at that worthy who in his embarrassment was scribbling nonsense on the foolscap sheet before him.

'Now because we have a black District Officer, we must pay oppressive taxes . . .' [6]

Momo simply has no conception that there is anything improper in the state of affairs he is describing. He has no notion of corruption or misappropriation of public funds. For him taxation is simply an arbitrary imposition from above, to be evaded as far as possible, or complied with under sufferance. Even the limited compliance which the villagers do afford to the authorities is not an encouraging sign. When they are obedient to the administration this is not out of responsible public spirit, but out of an abject and servile fear of the white man, as exasperating to Aluko (and the reader) as their stubborn defiance: 'We must do whatever the White Man says. He now owns Ipaja. He owns the world,' one Elder observed.' [7] And later Momo remarks: 'One more step and the White Man would become God'. [8] The villagers accord Akpan grudging respect because he is identified in their minds with the all-powerful whites. Indeed they constantly refer to him as 'the black White Man'.

Aluko thus, through vigorous caricature and broad comedy, highlights the key political problem facing Nigeria during this transition period. The old small-scale village system of responsibilities and loyalties has become inadequate in the context of the modern, impersonal nation-state which is in the process of being born. The people, however, particularly the older men, still cannot help seeing the world in terms of local customs and allegiances. And the situation is growing worse with the gradual withdrawal of the white man. At least the whites could impose an external, impartial and efficient order on society, by brute force if necessary. When the 'black white men' begin to take over, with the confusion of response this inevitably evokes in the people, chaos seems virtually inevitable. The analysis seems to lead to the conclusion that the British democratic system simply cannot work in the Nigeria of Aluko's day, or that it can be made to work only by the use of greater coercion than would be tolerated in Britain—in other words by ceasing to be democracy.

It is characteristic of Aluko that this problem should be seen in terms of comedy and satire, rather than tragedy. This is ensured by the drastic simplifications of focus which are central to Aluko's technique. By refusing to permit any dignity or pathos to the elders of Ipaja he excludes the more complex human dimensions of the situation which might interfere with his straightforwardly progressive and enlightened political interpretation. As it is, the villagers (with the partial exception of Ajayi, who is treated sketchily and killed off as soon as possible) remain delightfully exasperating caricatures, whose childlike antics continually interfere with Akpan's efforts to improve their lot. A similar simplification occurs in relation to the representative in the novel of intemperate nationalism, Benjamin Benjamin. The brief description of Benjamin's career which is given in the second chapter could be taken to imply that, had he not been unlucky, he might have achieved the same kind of position in society as Akpan himself. Expelled from his school because of a harmless love-letter just before taking his final examinations, and later, as a young journalist given a harsh prison sentence by a white judge for libelling the administration, Benjamin seems very much the victim of circumstance and colonial injustice. However, as soon as the novel's action begins to develop, all the potential human complexity of Benjamin's character is subsumed in Aluko's political purpose, and he becomes simply a caricature, if a splendidly vigorous one, of pretentiousness and half-educated deceit. Such simplifications of perspective

87

enable Aluko to present his material entirely in terms of practical politics, without any danger of confusion from emotional complexities or conflicting political viewpoints. Also, on a more practical level, it ensures that the reader's self-identification remains with Akpan, who otherwise would be in danger of becoming too obviously an authorial mouth-piece. Among such absurd and ridiculous caricatures Akpan appears, by contrast, as the representative of sanity and reason. And it would be an unresponsive reader indeed who failed to sympathise with his difficulties.

Akpan's problems do not all arise from the ignorance or wickedness of his fellow countrymen. Indeed on one level Aluko sees Akpan as a victim of white colonialism. It is Akpan's white superiors who let him down at the crucial moment in the novel's plot. While he has been attempting to impress upon the recalcitrant farmers that the *only* way to eradicate the cocoa disease is by felling all affected trees, the white authorities have been leaking news of a newly-discovered and less drastic cure to the newspapers, thus compromising his credibility and giving Benjamin a golden opportunity to accuse him of high-handedness and malice towards Ipaja. And then in the official report on the new cure the colonial authorities smugly congratulate themselves on this splendid achievement of British science. On seeing this report Akpan speaks, for all his 'moderate' views, with the voice of the most fervent nationalism.

'I am of the opinion that if that letter is any indication to go by, there is no self-respecting African who would want to identify himself with the present set-up.' [9]

It is important to notice however that, even at this point, Akpan is still nearer in political, social and cultural conscious-ness to his white superiors than to his fellow Africans. His anger at the colonial government is not on the level of ideology. There is no dispute over essentials. It is simply a response to what he sees as a failure of tact and correct procedure. Aluko underlines this by showing that Stanfield, the retiring District Officer, anticipates and sympathises with

Akpan's reaction to the self-congratulatory report from Westminster.

> He knew that Akpan had been little affected by the irresponsible nationalism around him. But he was an African and a patriot.[10]

And having made his point and demonstrated his protagonist's nationalism, Aluko allows Stanfield to 'get round' Akpan, and induce him to stay, responsibly, at his post.

In all essential matters then Akpan shares the mental landscape of the white characters. Indeed his own expressed views on the problems of government in Nigeria echo, not the moderate, meticulously democratic Stanfield, who is personally so sensitive to Akpan's difficulties; but rather Gregory, Stanfield's cynical colleague, who has little faith in the ability of Africans to cope with democracy. At the beginning of the novel Gregory states his case forcibly in opposition to Stanfield's liberalism.

> 'These bloody Africans need to be protected against themselves, and against their own ignorance. And damn it,' he continued, 'they need to be protected against our fancy notions of democracy. Just because we in Britain have evolved a system of government by discussion and argument which somehow seems to work we think we must see the same methods in tropical Africa. We think we must get agreement in every measure before we take decisions. But, what's the good of discussion by fellows who don't understand what we are talking about and persist in misunderstanding our motive?'[11]

Although Stanfield insists in reply on due democratic process, and is portrayed by Aluko as the better man, it is Gregory's lesson that the book teaches, and it is Gregory's views that Akpan has adopted in the long discussion with which the novel closes. Benjamin Benjamin, he says, would be harmless enough in a British context. He would speak at Hyde Park Corner and provide amusement for ice-cream eating Yorkshire housewives on holiday in London. His ideas there would be ignored among all the myriad other ideas allowed by 'free speech'.

89

'But it is an entirely different thing in this country where the masses, illiterate and ignorant, believe everything that anyone that can read and write tells them.' [12]

Thus Akpan, for all his nationalism, is ideologically a product of his colonial superiors. And, what is more, he places himself well to the right in the spectrum of colonial opinion.

The real villain in Aluko's world still remains, not the departing colonist, from whom, despite his faults, so much has been learned, but the ignorance and stupidity of the people. Aluko's view—that it is the mulish inertia of the rural peasantry which is the chief obstacle to political progress—is of course similar to that of Marx. Aluko's perspective is however very different from that of the Marxist or neo-Marxist. The lesson he teaches is not politicisation and revolution, but the strengthening of existing authority. The reason for this is not hard to find. Aluko's position is not, despite his show of balanced argument, that of a detached analyst of the social structure. It is that of a member of the new ruling class. And for all his genuine concern for the future of his country, it is not difficult to see that he envisages this future very much on his own elitist terms. He is a kind of Nigerian tory. He and other 'educated men' like him will govern, as enlightened patricians, in the best interests of all. Since the novel is set in 1949 the luxuries and material benefits of Akpan's status do not strike the reader as forcibly as they might in a novel set later. But they are highly significant nevertheless. And Aluko's treatment of them shows great relish. Sometimes Akpan seems to be preening himself on his sophistication and European sense of style.

Lounging in his white trousers and polo shirt after supper the day after Josiah Olaiya's visit, Udo Akpan began to go through the day's papers. [13]

The words are laden with the implication that this is a 'new man', an African version of the European 'executive type'. Even the name of his meal, 'supper', has the correct British social nuance. Akpan (and Aluko) clearly enjoy the wide-eyed amazement of the poor village pastor as he wonders 'that an African like himself could live in such splendour'.[14] Akpan casually offers the clergyman cocktails, ordering his servant, in the colonial style prevalent in Nigeria to this day, to bring 'drinks for two masters'.[15] There is no hint of irony or criticism in Aluko's tone here. And it cannot but seem that Gakwandi's verdict is just:

> ...all he wishes to see is a few men of integrity stepping into the shoes of the colonial administrators.[16]

A political philsophy which stresses the need to keep the unruly populace firmly in check and strengthen the power of the new elite, is suspiciously convenient in a novelist who so relishes his protagonist's privileges and the glamour of his social status.

Such doubts may lead us to re-examine Akpan's difficulties with the villagers of Ipaja. It may seem significant that Aluko, alone among Nigerian writers, can find nothing but ignorance and superstition in traditional life. We may begin to ask if after all the villagers are so wrong to distrust this 'black white man'. It cannot be denied that in practical and technological matters his is the voice of progress. But, urgent though these matters were and are in Nigeria, there are social and cultural dimensions to the life of any community which are of equal, if not greater, importance. Are the villagers wrong to distrust a man set over them who owns a car, eats 'supper' and drinks cocktails, has an elitist notion of his superiority over the illiterate and ignorant 'masses', and speaks to them in the language of the white man? Aluko has failed here in basic class-awareness. In his consciousness of good intensions and his impatient idealism he fails to see that the antagonism between the people and the administrators is *not* simply the result of an ignorant recalcitrance on the part of the ruled, nor of an unfortunate failure of communication on the part of the rulers: a matter of 'misunderstood motives'. It is a conflict of real interests between two social classes. With his focus firmly on the practicalities of taxation, water-supply and agricultural management Aluko avoids seeing the human and social aspects of government as anything more than complications in the path of material progress. He never confronts the fact that for all Akpan's good intentions, his class—the administrators, lawyers and surveyors in the novel—is drawing all the material benefits society can offer; while the Momos and Ajayis have nothing comparable to show for the supposed 'progress' of their society. This is why Akpan is, in the final analysis, an implausible figure. The facile marriage in his characterisation between on the one hand his personal affluence, his European style and sophistication, and on the other his high, public-spirited moral tone and nationalistic fervour, just does not hold together. In the social and economic realities of Nigeria at this time the two must conflict. And in the more subtle treatments of Aluko's themes which we find in the works of Achebe, this is exactly what does happen.

This then is one of that large group of novels, the value-system of which many readers will feel it necessary to turn inside out. Aluko's perspective presents us with an enlightened and patriotic new African administrator, undermined on the one hand by the high-handed colonialists, and thwarted on the other by the ignorant masses. But as we have seen the seditious reader can find ample evidence in the novel for a reinterpretation. Such a reader may see in Momo and his followers more than the caricatures Aluko makes of them. They could be seen on a different political analysis, as the unintended heroes of the novel, assailed from one side by their new colonial master, the smug 'black white man', and from the other by the bogus demagoguery of opportunists such as Benjamin Benjamin. And it is perhaps, after all, a tribute to the complexity of the book's realism that, despite its glaring faults, it does supply the reader within its pages with the material for such reinterpretations: that it can be felt to contradict itself so comprehensively.

# 4 'Distress and difficulty': Chinua Achebe

If Aluko is still in Fanon's first phase of colonial and post-colonial literature, the phase of 'unadulterated assimiliation', then Achebe is the classic representative in Nigeria of the second. According to Fanon:

> In the second phase we find the native is disturbed; he decides to remember what he is ... Past happenings of the bygone days of childhood will be brought up out of the depths of his memory ... Sometimes this literature of just-before-the-battle is dominated by humour and by allegory; but often too it is symptomatic of a period of distress and difficulty, where death is experienced, and disgust too. [1]

Two of Achebe's novels (*Things Fall Apart* (1958) and *Arrow of God* (1964)) seek to reconstruct the pre-colonial world from memories of his village childhood, and show that concern with origins which Fanon sees as an essential stage in the 'native's' search for identity. Achebe's other two novels deal directly with contemporary social and political problems, the 'distress and difficulty' to which Fanon refers being clearly expressed in the title of the first, *No Longer At Ease* (1960). This novel shows obvious parallels with *One Man, One Matchet*, but its emphasis is quite different, and the easy shelving of problems which occurs in Aluko's novel, is absent here. Obi, Achebe's representative of the new elite, is, like Akpan, caught between the remnants of colonialism and his ill-educated fellow countrymen. But the novel is set in 1958-9 rather than in 1949. The situation has become more complex and ambiguous with the imminence of the withdrawal of the white

93

administration. Moreover Achebe's ironic viewpoint denies the reader the simple approval of the protagonist which we found in Aluko. Obi is forced to pay for his 'European' status, as the logic of neo-colonialism dictates, by a descent into corruption and a loss of his sense of identity.

*A Man of the People* (1966) takes the problem into the more public arena of party-politics and treats the familiar theme of the gulf between the educated elite and the mass of the electorate. In one sense this novel could be said to fulfil the dire warnings of Aluko. In *One Man, One Matchet* disaster was avoided only by accident. The demagogue, Benjamin, was conveniently murdered by a local chieftain while at the height of his popularity, thus leaving power safely in the hands of 'educated men'. This murder which occurs because Benjamin has been committing adultery with one of the chief's wives, is quite irrelevant to the novel's political theme. Benjamin is, in fact, never defeated politically in the novel. With Achebe's more consistent treatment of the theme there are no such fortunate accidents. In Achebe's world the Benjamins have, as the real logic of Aluko's novel suggests they will, seized the political power formerly held by the whites, while the 'honest educated' men are reduced, like Odili, to the status of alienated and embittered hangers-on. The perceptive, educated protagonist feels his intelligence powerless and his honesty compromised between the half-educated demagogue, Nanga (a more subtle version of Benjamin), and Nanga's willing dupes, the ignorant populace. But Achebe's political vision is not simply a more pessimistic version of Aluko's. In his view the problem is not, as Aluko would feel, simply a matter of the wrong class of people having seized power. Achebe's educated Nigerian is portrayed with doubts and ironies unknown to the older writer. Odili's motives seem dubious even to himself, while Max, Odili's politician friend, actually defends the practice of taking bribes. So, although Achebe shares Aluko's conviction that education and personal honesty are the essential requisites for Nigeria's progress, he does not assume that the one entails the other, nor does he locate these qualities in any clearly identifiable social group or class. In short, Aluko, a civil servant, writes novels which promote the interests of his class; while Achebe, a novelist proper, analyses social and political life through a concrete realisation of the contradictions and ambiguities of individual experience. His answers are consequently not so easy as Aluko's.

## 'No Longer At Ease' (1960)

Although *No Longer At Ease* is by no means intended as allegory it is easy to see the career of Obi, its protagonist, as paradigmatic. He typifies on the individual level the situation of the Nigerian state as a whole. Europe has superimposed on many local loyalties the modern nation-state identity of Nigeria. So also Obi, as a representative modern Nigerian has buried his village loyalties under a European education and an idealistic conception of the individual's duty to the new state. As the naive poem 'Nigeria', written during his time in England shows, Obi is determined to maintain this conception of his own integrity—detribalised, free from superstition, thoroughly modern. But Europe has not only given Nigeria and Obi their new political ideals. It has also given them access to irresistible material goods. The people of Nigeria demand of their leaders an immediate supply of European comfort, convenience and luxury. And similarly, on the individual level, the people of Obi's village, represented by The Umuofia People's Progressive Union, demand of him, their educated, Europeanised son, the benefits to which his education has given him access. But, on the national level, Nigeria's own industry and commerce are not sufficiently developed to supply the people's demands. While on the individual level Obi's civil service income is not sufficient to satisfy his fellow villagers. So Obi must do as the nation which he typifies does: he must live beyond his means. He can see that insolvency is bound to result from such lavish expenditure without any solid base in capital. But the social pressure upon him is too great. He is trapped.

The Umuofia People's Progressive Union, unaware of the wider problems of economics and still seeing the world entirely in terms of local and immediate needs, conceives of Obi as an investment which must be made to pay off. They have saved to pay for his education and now he must repay the debt: not only literally, but also in all kinds of less tangible ways. As the Chairman says on Obi's return from Britain:

> 'We are happy that today we have such an invaluable possession in the person of our illustrious son and guest of honour.'
> He traced the history of the Umuofia Scholarship Scheme which had made it possible for Obi to study overseas, and called it an investment which must yield heavy dividends.[2]

One of the more indirect ways in which Obi is expected to repay his debt to the village is by keeping up a life of conspicuous expenditure. The villagers demand such ostentation as a means of enhancing their own prestige, and as a visible proof of Obi's 'European' status.

> To occupy a 'European post' was second only to actually being a European. It raised a man from the masses to the élite whose small talk at cocktail parties was: 'How's the car behaving?'[3]

Obi's course if he is to continue as society demands is corruption or massive debt. And this on the national level is the way taken by the governments of most developing countries. On the one hand there is conspicuous expenditure on prestige projects. (The recently completed Lagos International Trade Fair complex has been criticised as such an extravagance.)[4] On the other hand the real wealth-producing potential of the nation is mortgaged or sold, often corruptly, to foreign interests in return for local or transient benefits. At every point then Obi can be seen to be acting out on the private level the larger political compromises and failures of the nation itself.

At one point Obi considers adopting on his individual level the equivalent of the national policy of an Algeria or a Tanzania: severe retrenchment and a determination to avoid insolvency by living as far as possible within his means. But as

96

Achebe wittily shows, this is, in simple human terms, quite impossible for a man in his position in Nigerian society.

> Having made him a member of an exclusive club whose members greet one another with 'How's the car behaving?' did they expect him to turn round and answer: 'I'm sorry, but my car is off the road. You see I couldn't pay my insurance premium.'? That would be letting the side down in a way that was quite unthinkable. Almost as unthinkable as a masked spirit in the old Ibo society answering another's esoteric salutation: 'I'm sorry, my friend, but I don't understand your strange language. I'm but a human being wearing a mask.' No, these things could not be. [5]

It is characteristic of Achebe's subtle vision that he images this impossibility in terms of traditional ritual. For all the apparent differences, he implies, the taboos of modern Nigeria are no less absolute and peremptory than those of previous ages. Moreover Nigeria is a syncretic society in which (as Peil shows) apparently 'modern' concepts are often fitted into the older framework without any real change of overall consciousness. For Achebe then, Obi's is an inevitable tragedy; he is a victim of social and political forces beyond his control. 'It seemed that was the way Nigeria was built.' [6]

Here Achebe's viewpoint differs markedly from that of a revolutionary political ideologist such as Frantz Fanon, although his analysis of the situation is essentially the same as Fanon's. Fanon of course would not allow Obi's tragedy to be inevitable. To him Obi would illustrate the powerlessness of the under-developed bourgeoisie to achieve the revolution of consciousness necessary for a political change. This revolution must however still take place. If Nigeria is 'built' this way then it must be dismantled and rebuilt differently. Obi, and the Nigerian ruling elite which he typifies, must break with their dependent post-colonial ideology, whether they possess the will to do so or not. The client status must be rejected.

> Europe has laid her hands on our contents and we must slash at her fingers till she lets go. [7]

Achebe however as a novelist primarily concerned with re-

alising the individual complexities in the life of one member
of the elite, cannot see things in these terms. He is too painfully aware that the *homme moyen sensuel* such as Obi, far
from slashing at Europe's fingers, cannot help but cling to
them with eager tenacity, urged on by the Umuofia People's
Progressive Union and all that it stands for in Nigerian society.
The novel sees the situation from within his consciousness,
and seems to pose the question: who can blame him? Obi is
clearly meant to gain the reader's sympathy.

The strength of this novel lies in its realisation of the
psychological and moral impact of Nigerian society on the
mind of one rather ordinary member of the elite. It offers no
political prescriptions. Rather it fleshes out the basic political
and social realities with dramatic incident and particularised
detail. Obi's career thus stands as an exemplum, a typical
Nigerian case, while still retaining the quality of lived personal
experience. The reader is always intimately involved in, even
identified with, Obi's responses, and is thus made to experience the social pressures to which he is subjected, at first
hand. Seeing a lorry driver about to bribe a traffic policeman
for instance, Obi catches the latter's eye and the bribe is not
paid. But, to Obi's and the reader's surprise, instead of being
grateful to him for saving the money and asserting moral
right, the driver and the lorry's passengers berate him for his
interference. Indeed the driver's mate has to run back with
an even larger bribe so as to avoid being victimised by the
police in revenge. Obi's morally right action has only complicated the corruption and made it worse. It is the ironic
humour in such episodes, so characteristic of Achebe, which
gives them their dramatic force and lends authenticity to his
larger pessimistic conclusions about society.

The whole structure of the novel indeed can be seen to
rely on similar ironies to that in the episode of the lorry
driver. A web of contradictory social demands is shown to
surround Obi, of such complexity that his attempts to hold
on to his ideals seem virtually comic. The reader is appalled
and at the same time cannot help but laugh with a kind of
helpless exasperation, at Obi's impossible plight. It is for

instance precisely his education in Europe which makes him so idealistic in his determination to serve the new nation-state with selfless devotion. While it is ironically this same education which qualifies him for the post in the bureaucracy that both makes a life of conspicuous expenditure a social necessity, and puts him in a position to practise corruption profitably. Again, it is his European education which makes him so contemptuously reject the taboo against marrying the *osu* or outcast, Clara. While those to whom he is indebted for this education, the villagers of Umuofia, are ironically the sternest upholders of the taboo. After his quarrel with the Umuofia People's Progressive Union over this issue Obi vows to repay the money spent on his education as quickly as possible, a decision the reader cannot fail to respect, but one which, in his insolvent state, is bound to sap his resistance to the taking of bribes. Harassed on all sides by these contradictory pressures Obi's situation is both comically absurd and tragically inescapable. The idea of himself which he has brought back from Europe cannot survive such a bombardment. He even reflects at one point that he can never be sure that, despite his efforts to preserve his integrity, a brother or a 'friend' might not all the time have been taking bribes 'on his behalf', pretending to be his agent. Undermined by such ironies Obi's self-respect inevitably crumbles, his very sense of identity begins to crack. He gives up the struggle and succumbs to corruption.

## 'A Man of the People' (1966)

*A Man of the People* is more explicitly concerned with politics than *No Longer At Ease*, and indeed has established itself as the classic Nigerian 'political novel'. The source of its wider political perspective lies in its protagonist, who uniquely in Achebe's novels is also the first person narrator. Where Obi was something of an *ingénu*, an innocent victim of society, Odili is self-aware and articulate, conscious of larger political issues and capable of analysing them for the reader. It is the voice of Odili, with its wry, self-mocking humour (not very different from Achebe's own narrative voice) which controls the reader's response to the events of the novel. It also gives what must stand as the most memorable description in all literature of the post-colonial elite.

> A man who has just come in from the rain and dried his body and put on dry clothes is more reluctant to go out again than another who has been indoors all the time. The trouble with our new nation —as I saw it then lying on the bed—was that none of us had been indoors long enough to be able to say 'To hell with it'. We had been in the rain together until yesterday. Then a handful of us—the smart and the lucky and hardly ever the best—had scrambled for the one shelter our former rulers left, and had taken it over and barricaded themselves in. And from within they sought to persuade the rest through numerous loudspeakers, that the first phase of the struggle had been won and that the next phase—the extension of our house— was even more important and called for new and original tactics; it required that all argument should cease and the whole people speak with one voice and that any more dissent and argument outside the door of the shelter would subvert and bring down the whole house. [8]

The image is nicely resonant. And the fact that it comes to us from the luxury of one of Chief Nanga's seven well-appointed bedrooms underlines with neat irony the 'treason of the clerks' committed by the Nigerian intelligentsia which Odili represents.

It is important to stress the complexity of Odili's narrative voice, since influential critics have sought to simplify Odili's role and thus also reduce the novel's political dimension. Eustace Palmer [9] and Gareth Griffiths[10] both see Odili as a corrupt man and an unreliable narrator. Intelligent and witty though he is, they feel that he is tainted by his contact with Nanga and that his judgement is therefore unreliable. Moreover they deny that his involvement in politics is a genuine political act, explaining it almost entirely in terms of personal motives: at first simple greed and later the desire to revenge himself on Nanga for stealing his girlfriend, Elsie. To Palmer the portrayal of Odili shows the corruption of a young man by wealth. There is nothing favourable he can find to say

about Odili on any level. He mentions Odili's 'inept' punc-
tuation (a strange point) and 'stylistic infelicities',[11] quoting
examples of perfectly acceptable, if racy, English to support
his argument; and implies that Odili's vulgar and arrogant
character is the subject of consistent irony on the author's
part. He talks of the 'hollowness' of Odili's mind and con-
cludes roundly:

> Odili probably ranks as one of Achebe's most unpleasant characters.
> He is lecherous, egoistic, vulgar, shallow-minded in spite of his
> college education and ready to criticise others . . . [12]

Such prim censure as this does great violence to the actual
complex effect of Odili on the responsive reader. Palmer
rightly says that Odili's function in the novel is a dual one,
both as victim of corruption and commentator on it.

> Achebe needs great technical virtuosity and control to use Odili both
> as his mouthpiece against corruption, and to expose Odili's own
> susceptibility to corruption. He must look through Odili's eyes at
> society, but also stand apart from him, observing him critically. [13]

But this stress on the detachment of the author from his
protagonist is mistaken. It ignores the crucial fact that the
ironies directed at Odili come not direct from the author, but
from Odili himself. It is he who exposes *his own* 'susceptibility to corruption' for the reader. Palmer remarks that
after his first meeting with Nanga Odili's 'judgements cannot
be relied upon'.[14] This is the opposite of the truth. Throughout the novel Odili's judgement is the only reliable point of
reference: all the more reliable because its harshest verdicts
are often passed on Odili himself. The irony and criticism
are not directed in the first place by the author against the
character, as Palmer says, but by the character against himself.
Odili's political actions and his comments on politics are thus
far more complex and interesting than Palmer's version
would allow.

The character of Odili is a most subtle device for exploring
the relation between ideals and reality, the moral world and
the world of politics. His underlying integrity and high ideals

101

never waver, while he continually points out to the reader the failure of himself and of his whole society to achieve such integrity in practice. His characteristic tone is one of self-distrust. Throughout the opening scene Odili observes himself and his reactions to Nanga with a rueful eye, wincing now and then at his own weakness. For instance when Nanga singles him out for special notice:

> 'Well,' I said happily—I'm ashamed to admit. 'I know how busy a minister . . .' [15]

And when later he shouts 'hear, hear' to some flattering banality from the Senior Tutor, he comments wryly: 'I like to think that I meant it to be sarcastic.' [16] These remarks are those of a refined and self-critical intelligence, not of the shallow-minded egotistical rogue of Palmer's version. It is important also to realise that, despite his susceptibility, Odili remains in all essential respects, honest throughout the novel. When he begins to understand that Edna, Nanga's proposed second wife, whom he is trying to seduce in revenge, is not a mere sex-object, but a vulnerable human being worthy of affection, he is thoroughly chastened and self-disgusted. His basic respect for others defeats his youthful arrogance (and what Palmer would call his 'lecherousness'). On the political level, he refuses ever to take a bribe, even when the transaction could easily have passed undetected. In this he is unique in a novel where society is built on bribery and corruption. That this interpretation of Odili as a sensitive, if rather callow young man, learning about himself and about life as the novel goes on, corresponds with the author's intention, can be seen from Achebe's remarks on this subject, recorded by Bernth Lindfors.

> Well, I like that young man. He was idealistic, he was naïve, he was this and he was that, but I think he was also basically honest, which makes a difference. He was very honest. He knew his own short-comings; he even knew when his motives were not very pure. This puts him in a class worthy of attention, as far as I'm concerned. [17]

Not only is Odili an honest observer of himself and others, he is also a man with a serious interest in public affairs who has followed the larger political development of his new nation from its inception. It is implied in the first few pages that he has always had ambitions to play a useful part himself in practical politics. Odili's reflections on Nanga and his success in public life then, are those of an idealistic and perceptive young man becoming increasingly alienated in a society which seems to offer no hope of a realisation of his ideals. It is certainly not a simple process of individual corruption which occurs in this first chapter. It has wider implications. Odili can be seen as representing the youthful idealism of a generation, undermined by the endemic corruption of his society. Odili begins by relating the disgust he felt in the early days at the cynical witch hunt against the more highly educated members of parliament with which Nanga began his career. He is fascinated as well as horrified by Nanga's success. And his motives being, as always, mixed, he is also envious of Nanga's undeniable political skills. The opening scene at the school illustrates this confusion of attitudes. Odili is at first simply disgusted by the crude enthusiasm of the populace for Nanga. His disgust turns to contempt for the people and a despairing cynicism, disguised as insouciance. In this confused state of mind he is swept up in Nanga's glamour, although, significantly, even at this point he still remembers his ideals.

> I knew I ought to be angry with myself but I wasn't. I found myself wondering whether—perhaps—I had been applying to politics stringent standards that didn't belong to it.[18]

Nigeria at this time, he reflects, cannot support honesty in politics. The moral is that politics is the art of the possible, and with crude materials only crude methods will meet with success.

> Somehow I found myself admiring the man for his lack of modesty. For what is modesty but inverted pride? We all think we are first-class people. Modesty forbids us from saying so ourselves though, presumably, not from wanting to hear it from others. Perhaps it was their impatience with this kind of hypocrisy that made men like Nanga successful politicians while starry-eyed idealists strove vaingloriously

103

to bring into politics niceties and delicate refinements that belonged elsewhere. [19]

There is something very painful about Odili's awareness of his own compromises during this first scene. His analysis seems only too accurate; and it is a natural response to what he depicts to take refuge in cynicism. But his yielding to cynicism remains partial and unconvincing despite all his rationalisations. 'Perhaps' is one of his key terms.

Throughout the first half of the novel Odili's hesitant compromises with Nanga's corruption and the larger analysis of Nigerian society which emerges through them, make this the most interesting political novel Nigeria has yet produced. However this success is not sustained. All the most complex and coherent analyses of issues occur in this first half. As soon as Odili quarrels with Nanga and goes into politics proper, as a member of Max's party, the pace of the novel speeds up disconcertingly and much subtlety is lost. Palmer's judgement that 'Odili's primary motive in entering politics is revenge',[20] seems to gain ample support from the text. Achebe apparently abandons the political issues which occupied him up to this point, and the novel instead recounts a squabble between two men over a woman. The immediate cause of Odili's leaving Nanga's house has nothing to do with politics; it is Nanga's theft of Elsie, Odili's girlfriend. Odili joins Max's opposition party the next day, in retaliation as it were. And thereafter the political theme of the novel seems virtually reduced to one aspect of Odili's personal quarrel with Nanga. On the personal level Odili seeks revenge by attempting to seduce Nanga's proposed second wife, Edna, while in the public arena he revenges himself by standing against Nanga in the election. After the subtle exploration of political life in the first few chapters, this sudden reduction of the action to the level of a personal vendetta is most unfortunate. And it can scarcely have been intended by Achebe to have so crude an effect.

A close examination of the text reveals that the political theme *is* still there. Max's political ideas, sketchily as they are described, do answer to Odili's original aspirations. And the incident in which Odili refuses Nanga's bribe is presented in such a way as to suggest that Odili is still as concerned with asserting integrity in public life as with revenging himself on Nanga. But the political element of the book has become fragmented and incoherent just at the point when it should have begun to develop new dimensions with the introduction of Max, Eunice and the new political party. The way Odili is projected out of Nanga's house by the quarrel over Elsie, straight into the neatly contrasted ideological world of Max, is too much a matter of plot-manipulation. There should be an ideological cause for his shift of allegiance. And the whole of the political discussion between Max and the others in Chapter Eight is vague. A welter of plot-developments follows thick and fast and drowns reflection. Achebe takes the easy way out, relying on the primary passions of personal love and hate between individuals to carry the book on. Odili falls in love with Edna, then is beaten up at Nanga's meeting; Max is killed by Koko's thugs, only to be revenged immediately when Eunice shoots Koko himself. The novel, which began as a most ambitious study of Nigerian politics, ends in the melodrama of purely personal confrontations. And finally, like an old-fashioned *deus ex machina*, the army, hitherto scarcely mentioned in the novel, steps in, and a military *coup* brings the action to an abrupt end.

This failure in the novel cannot however be condemned simply as a technical blemish, the result of carelessness or haste. As often happens with the work of a real artist, the technique of the novel, even in its failures, tells us something valuable about its subject. The replacement of the complex techniques of psychological analysis and ironic juxtaposition by the crudities of violent plot-development and breathless narrative could be said to be a necessary consequence of the novel's ambitious theme—Nigeria being what it was in the mid-1960s. The logic of the story Achebe tells dictates no natural resolution in the political terms of party-politics within which Nanga, Max and Odili all operate. Similarly the literary complexity of Odili's early analytical style is over-taken by developments on the public scene whose crudity

105

makes such subtle analysis pointless. Corruption is so general and the level of political consciousness among the electorate is so low, that any suggestion of a purely 'political' answer to the problems of Nigeria, or of any plausible programme of political action, is impossible. The chaos cannot but become worse and worse, until the system itself is swept away. This is why Achebe finds it impossible to put any imaginative energy into his description of Max's party and its policies, and why they remain such shadowy elements in the novel. Odili himself has pointed out a related and more obvious reason: that he, Max and the others are simply 'starry-eyed idealists', out of touch with the people. On this reading the military *coup* which ends the novel is inevitable and not simply a *deus ex machina*, a mechanical plot-device to extricate the author from a situation to which he can see no organic resolution. In the event, of course, art anticipated the crude plot-devices of life itself, and within less than a month of the book's publication in January 1966 the gordian knot of contradictions within democratic, parliamentary Nigeria was indeed cut by a *coup*. It was even suspected by non-Ibos that Achebe knew of the *coup* in advance and deliberately anticipated it in the novel—a naive and unnecessary deduction.[21] The situation diagnosed by Achebe could not plausibly have been resolved in any less drastic or violent way—either in the novel or in life itself.

The crux of the problem as Achebe sees it is a more complex version of that we found in Aluko; the inappropriateness in Nigeria of an imposed democratic system whose aims and principles are not understood, or if understood not supported, by the vast majority of the populace. Odili constantly laments the narrowness of vision of the people, particularly the older generation. Towards the end of the novel Odili's father sums up the career of the corrupt politician, Koko, in terms of a traditional proverb. Koko deserved his fate, he says, because he had 'taken enough for the owner to see'. In other words self-seeking is natural and proper as long as it remains discreet and moderate—as long as the 'owner' doesn't see. Odili finds his father's old-fashioned morality grotesquely meaningless, and also ominous, in the new circumstances of modern Nigeria.

> My father's words struck me because they were the very same words the villagers of Anata had spoken of Josiah, the abominated trader. Only in their case the words had meaning. The owner was the village, and the village had a mind; it could say no to sacrilege. But in the affairs of the nation there was no owner, the laws of the village became powerless. [22]

Conflict between private advantage and the public good is of course a universal problem. Public property and public money are everywhere stolen with less qualms than private. But in a country such as Nigeria in the 1960s the problem is particularly acute because the very conception of the wider national interest and the political institutions which promote that interest—even the notion of the state itself—are ill-understood by a population still thinking, like Odili's father, in traditional village terms.

Odili frequently refers to the 'cynicism' of the people, who support politicians like Nanga knowing them to be givers and takers of bribes. But Achebe's treatment makes it clear that this 'cynicism' is not so much a failure of morality as the application of an older but perfectly coherent and practical morality to a situation where it is no longer appropriate.

> Our people say that if you pay homage to the man at the top others will pay homage to you when it is your turn to be on top. Well that is what the old men say. [23]

In a small village community this is excellent wisdom. It ensures social cohesion, and controls jealousies and resentments. Moreover, since the positions of wealth and authority are comparatively limited, firstly by a subsistence rural economy and secondly by traditional custom, its stress on personal aggrandisement cannot threaten the well-being of society as a whole. Transplanted into the huge, impersonal nation-state which Nigeria had become by this time however, it can only result in the advancement of individuals at the expense of the public good. The 'man at the top' is no longer

107

a local dignitary, personally known to his whole society and with clear bonds of physical relationship or custom between him and all the others. He is a public servant, whose duty is to the abstraction of 'the state' and through the state to thousands or millions of his compatriots, who will be from different ethnic groups, and very few of whom he will ever meet. He may also be in a position to control vast national resources. It is clear that in this context the old, personalised system of 'homage' and patronage must manifest itself as bribery and corruption on a massive scale. The modern democratic state relies for survival on the observance of, or at least lip-service to, certain highly abstract ideals: public accountability of politicians and civil servants, freedom of the individual, free speech, acceptance of democratically reached decisions. All these are mocked and undermined by the homely wisdom of Odili's father.

> He took the view (without expressing it in so many words) that the mainspring of political action was personal gain, a view which, I might say, was much more in line with the general feeling in the country than the high-minded thinking of fellows like Max and I.[24]

Achebe's analysis is thus far an amplification of Aluko's. He differs essentially from Aluko however in his greater under-standing of, and feeling for, the traditional view. He shows clearly that no-one is to blame, setting down the tragic contra-dictions of the situation without crudely taking sides. Odili's father's philosophy is often expressed in a down-to-earth, mellow way which makes it seem more attractive than Odili's tart modernity. Much of the humour of the novel derives from it: 'they would ask you—as my father did—if you thought that a sensible man would spit out the juicy morsel that good fortune placed in his mouth.'[25] The reader is almost less inclined to sympathise with Odili than to accuse him of intellectual snobbery when he condemns the crowds collected to see Nanga as 'not only ignorant but cynical'.[26] It is nonetheless clear however that in Achebe's view this older morality must be superseded if the political system is not to degenerate into chaos. It is essential that the new morality which Odili represents, with its abstract and difficult ideals, should gain acceptance. The reader is meant to admire Odili wholeheartedly for refusing Nanga's bribe, despite pressure from both the traditional African cynicism of his father and the Machiavellian European cynicism of Max, who both urge him to accept it. Achebe places himself firmly in the liberal humanist camp here, between a traditionalist right and an ideological left. When he learns that Max has taken Koko's bribe he remembers Nanga's reaction to his own refusal to accept one, and comments:

> The real point surely was that Max's action had jeopardised our moral position, our ability to inspire that kind of terror which I had seen so clearly in Nanga's eyes despite all his grandiloquent bluff, and which in the end was our society's only hope of salvation. [27]

Here, for once in the latter part of the novel, a political theme is treated with powerful dramatic conviction. For Achebe it is the connection between personal morality and political action which is the key to the future of society.

The fact that Odili remains unique in the novel in this vision of the road to Nigeria's salvation indicates Achebe's pessimism about its chances of achievement. This point needs emphasis since *A Man of the People* has been praised for its positive and progressive political outlook. J.P. O'Flinn in a generally stimulating essay on the Nigerian novel attempts to distinguish Achebe from his contemporaries on this basis. Okara, he says, suffers from the intellectual's 'disdain for the people',[28] Okolo's self-sacrifice being a useless and self-regarding gesture against corruption which achieves nothing. Soyinka, O'Flinn maintains, is similarly elitist. It is only Achebe who escapes this self-indulgent pessimism, arriving at the end of *A Man of the People* 'at an instinctive, tentative confidence in the "will of the whole people" '. 'It is here,' he continues, 'that Achebe moves beyond the spit in the eye of the nearest establishment figure with which Soyinka closes *The Interpreters*—a gesture of defiance, but scarcely of change.'[29] It is impossible to agree with O'Flinn that *A Man of the People* is so constructive a novel. As our analysis has

109

shown it is very difficult to see the *coup* which closes the novel as representing, however tentatively, 'the will of the whole people', except perhaps in a quite negative and destructive sense. Achebe's own view of the people's part in this event emerges clearly enough in the text, and has little in common with that of O'Flinn. There can be no doubt that Achebe agrees with Odili on this point.

> Some political commentators have said that it was the supreme cynicism of these transactions that inflamed the people and brought down the Government. That is sheer poppycock. The people themselves, as we have seen, had become even more cynical than their leaders and were apathetic into the bargain . . .
>
> No, the people had nothing to do with the fall of our Government. What happened was simply that unruly mobs and private armies having tasted blood and power during the election had got out of hand and ruined their masters and employers. And they had no public reason whatever for doing it. Let's make no mistake about that.[30]

Brutal, even cynical, as Odili's interpretation is, it carries more conviction in the context of the novel than O'Flinn's hopeful sentimentalism of 'an instinctive, tentative confidence in the "will of the whole people" '.

Indeed in all his novels Achebe frequently falls back on such shamelessly common-sense appeals to the basic faults of human nature, refusing to see everything in terms of correctable social engineering as strongly ideologically motivated writers tend to do. 'We ignore man's basic nature'[31] Odili says at one point, if we expect Nanga willingly to give up his privileges. And in *No Longer At Ease* Achebe fatalistically accepts the injustices of the world, both natural and man-made. 'Na so dis world be'[32] he quotes in pidgin. Often Odili's verdicts on Nanga's character make no mention of social or economic forces. It is simply a matter of human nature.

> Chief Nanga was a born politician; he could get away with almost anything he said or did. And as long as men are swayed by their hearts and stomachs and not their heads the Chief Nangas of this world will continue to get away with anything.[33]

Despite his awareness of political issues and his precise analyses of social attitudes Achebe, it seems, is unwilling to give an entirely ideologically committed diagnosis of Nigerian society. And the reader who prefers a more traditionally 'moral' interpretation of things to a 'political' one, will find ample support in Achebe. When the sixteen-year old Miss Marks in *No Longer At Ease* offers her body to Obi in return for his support on the Scholarship Board it is difficult to see neo-colonialism or any other factor peculiar to Nigeria in the 1960s as the primary culprit. Such 'sleeping one's way to the top' is surely commonplace in all societies, and has more to do with the age-old relation between the sexes than the tensions peculiar to a colonial society. Similarly Nanga's demagoguery and corruption, distinctly Nigerian in flavour as they are, are scarcely unfamiliar phenomena even in countries which have never experienced colonialism, or in the colonial nations themselves.

Achebe then gives a particularly subtle and complex version of the liberal humanist answer to the vexed question of the treatment of political themes in literary art. On the one hand he shows a keen awareness of the specific political and economic forces which dictate the problems of post-colonial Nigeria. On the other hand he refuses to interpret all human behaviour in terms of these forces: nor will he make direct equations between political positions and moral values, as more 'committed' writers do. He does full justice to the complexity of individual experience within the wider political context. His political analysis may be bleak. But his diagnosis in *A Man of the People*, with its lack of real solutions, carries a conviction which the very different optimisms of an O'Flinn or Fanon on the one hand, or an Aluko on the other, do not.


## 'The Voter' (1965)

One of the strongest aspects of *A Man of the People* is, as we have seen, its comic, yet sympathetic, realisation of the feelings of the mass of the electorate. The failure of the democratic party system is often more vividly explained by

111

an incidental detail than by explicit commentary. At Nanga's election rally for instance Odili notices the crowd's reaction to a microphone.

> A microphone was set up on the steps of the outhouse facing the crowd. What impressed them right away was how you could talk into that ball and get the voice thundering in a completely different place. 'Say what you will,' I heard someone remark, 'the white man is a spirit.' [34]

No explanation is necessary. It is clear enough that an elector whose responses are on this level can have no real conception of the democratic process in which he is participating and which the microphone is meant to facilitate.

But the most telling example of Achebe's empathy with the ordinary members of the electorate is to be found not in the novel, but in the related short story, *The Voter*. Here the focus falls not on a member of the intellectual elite, but on Roof, the lowly local agent of the candidate of the PAP (People's Alliance Party). The electorate has developed in political awareness to the point where it realises that the democratic system can be manipulated to its advantage. But people are not yet thinking on the level of policies for economic development or social welfare. Instead they simply demand the tangible individual benefit of a few shillings as payment for their votes at election time. Roof's job is to distribute this money, carefully adjusting the amount given to the social status of the particular elector. Roof's peace of mind is threatened when the opposition POP (Progressive Organisation Party) offers him five pounds for his own vote. By the values which govern the whole system within which he works, this offer is too good to be refused. And before he can stop himself he has sworn by a particularly powerful *iyi*, or juju, from Mbanta to vote for his employer's opponent.

> Roof's heart nearly flew out when he saw the *iyi*; indeed he knew the fame of Mbanta in these things. But he was a man of quick decision. What could a single vote cast in secret for Maduka take away from Marcus's certain victory? Nothing.
>
> 'I will cast my paper for Maduka; if not this *iyi* take note.'[35]

The confrontation here between traditional conceptions and the modern world is dramatic and delightfully witty.

The tension between Roof's two hired loyalties threatens to upset his composure as the time for him to cast his vote approaches. On the one hand he is paid by his employer to vote for him, and his ethnic loyalty also dictates that he do so. On the other hand he has been paid by Maduka to vote for him and has sworn an awesome vow to do so. It is clear that in this case the conception of voting as a process by which the elector selects the social and economic policies he feels best for the community is quite irrelevant. And in the event the actual physical casting of the vote neatly underlines this irrelevance.

> Quick as lightning a thought leapt into Roof's mind. He folded the paper, tore it in two along the crease and put one half in each box. He took the precaution of putting the first half into Maduka's box and confirming the action verbally: 'I vote for Maduka.'

> They marked his thumb with indelible purple ink to prevent his return, and he went out of the booth as jauntily as he had gone in.[36]

Thus he satisfies his traditional notions of loyalty by 'voting' for both his paymasters. But of course his vote is a spoilt one, and in the reality of democratic politics he has voted for no-one. This neat and masterly little story encapsulates one of the central points of *A Man of the People* with startling economy. With such an electorate democracy in the Nigeria of the 1960s is, as Achebe makes it appear, a farcical affair.

# 5 The artist and political commitment: Wole Soyinka

Soyinka is unique among Nigerian writers in his complexity—his unwillingness to confine himself to any single level of meaning or style. To the reader turning from Achebe his work may appear bewilderingly multi-dimensional. Clarity of statement frequently seems less important to Soyinka than faithfulness to the complexities and ambiguities of his apprehension of life. At times his very subject seems to be the indeterminateness of experience. As Gerald Moore says in relation to *The Interpreters*: 'A certain confusion of effect is necessary to Soyinka's purpose'.[1] People and events are seen in a multiplicity of simultaneous contexts: literal and metaphorical; individual, political, social, aesthetic, philosophical and religious. Yet, despite the apparently irreducible complexity of his world, he is always attempting to unify; like Ayi Kwei Armah and Christopher Okigbo he is a myth-maker. His work presents a constant struggle to draw his—indeed all human—experience into one all-embracing symbolic or mythical 'explanation'. Consequently, although few of his works lack a political dimension, it is impossible to separate his politics from his philosophy, aesthetics and religion. All are, at least in intention, unified in one complex world-view. While at the same time his diversity makes it difficult to pin him down to a consistent political position. His life and work give the impression of a passionately committed man. But to exactly what Soyinka is committed is sometimes obscure, even to himself—which is not to say that it is illusory or valueless.

Soyinka's refusal to simplify shows itself most clearly in

the almost obsessive determination of some of his work to make nonsense of conventional received ideas. One of his least problematical works, the comedy *The Lion and the Jewel*, relies on such an attack on comfortable stereotypes for much of its dramatic effect. At first we seem to be on familiar ground. The implications of the opening are clear enough. The innocent villagers, represented by the old chief and the village beauty, Sidi, with her ingenuous charm, are about to be corrupted by the modern world, which intrudes aggressively upon them in the persons of the flashy young schoolteacher, Lakunle, and the glamour-photographer from a Lagos magazine. In the event however this all too inviting interpretation reveals itself as a sentimentalism. The chief turns out to be a wily old operator who easily seduces Sidi away from Lakunle, using as a decoy an ultra-modern stamp-machine. Sidi emerges as, after all, a selfish and rather stupid narcissist. She becomes one of the ancient chief's many wives, taunting Lakunle with his lack of virility. Does the play then offer a celebration of the victory of healthy traditional values over slick modernity? If it does, it is an oddly wry one. Neither of the propagandist interpretations so strongly evoked by the story can in fact be made to fit. A similar undermining of expected sterotypes is apparent in *The Interpreters*. The most prominent white in the novel, Monica, approximates to no familiar post-colonial type. She is the sensitive, long-suffering, if rather gauche wife of a snobbish and overbearing black boor. Again, the apostle of Négritude in the novel, Joe Golder, is a quarter-negro American who has come to Africa in search of his roots and in order to blacken his skin, a process he helps along with a sun-lamp. To compound the irreducible individuality of his situation, he is also a homosexual. The religious theme of the book centres on Lazarus, a charismatic revivalist preacher who happens also to be an albino—a white black. Examples could be multiplied, but the point is clear. The crude and self-indulgent myths which we impose on real life fail to do justice to its inexhaustible variety.

This complexity of content is expressed through an equal complexity of styles and techniques. Soyinka has written poems, plays (tragic, comic and tragicomic), novels and essays. His work ranges in style from the involved metaphysical rhetoric of *Myth, Literature and the African World* (1976) to the brisk farce of *The Trials of Brother Jero* (1964); from the lyrical mysticism of *Idanre* (1967) to the interior analyses of *The Interpreters* (1965). Often he mixes styles within the same work: a realistically portrayed character suddenly revealing a symbolic dimension, or a moment of high tragedy being undercut by a flippant pun. Early in his career he was nicknamed the Nigerian Bernard Shaw [2] on the strength of such works as *The Lion and the Jewel*. But in other works a bewildering variety of parallels and influences makes his stylistic repertoire one of the largest of any contemporary writer. Echoes of Shakespeare, Samuel Beckett, Ibsen, Chekhov, Dickens, Joyce, Solzhenitsyn, Nietzsche and George Wilson Knight are all digested in his work. And notwithstanding, or rather because of, this variety of influences, his voice is always distinct and individual. He is an astounding assimilative talent.

It is not surprising, in view of this breadth of subject and assured eclecticism of style, that Soyinka should have been dubbed by some critics a 'world writer'. Bernth Lindfors wrote in 1975: 'His imagination, vision and craft distinguish him as a creative artist of the very first rank, as a writer of world stature. Some would say he is the only truly original literary genius that Africa has yet produced.' [3] Soyinka himself has invited such a 'world' perspective on his work, insisting that he is not *merely* an African writer, and that his themes are common to all humanity. In 1969 he remarked (with typical rhetoric): 'the situation in Africa today is the same as in the rest of the world; it is not one of the tragedies which come of isolated human failures but the very collapse of humanity.' [4] On the other hand, he was quick to object when he felt that this 'universality' was being used in a kind of ideological neo-colonialism, to deny the real Africanness of his writing. Though by no means a Négritudinist, reacting against white racism with black racism, Soyinka insists that he and his fellow writers *do* share a common African worldview.

. . . it has been with an increasing sense of alarm and even betrayal that we have watched our position distorted and exploited to embrace a 'sophisticated' school of thought which (for ideological reasons) actually repudiates the existence of an African world![5]

Such an unwillingness to allow his ideological position to be simplified is characteristic of Soyinka. In some cases, as we shall see, it may be felt to border on wilful perversity.

Faced with the intimidating subtlety of Soyinka's mind and the virtuosity of his style, critics range themselves broadly into two ideological camps: the traditional 'literary critical' and the committed left. The commentator grounded in the British literary critical tradition may yield to a tendency towards pious overpraise. At its most extreme it seems as if to proclaim the advent of a truly original literary genius in Africa were sufficient to discharge the critical task, and to qualify or analyse further would be bad manners. The piety of such critics is clearest in their approach to Soyinka's celebrated obscurity. Confronted by the welter of plot-complications and the superabundance of allegorical figures towards the end of *A Dance of the Forests* (1960) for instance, Eldred Jones, intimidated, leaves the problem for posterity to sort out.

> Each succeeding reading produces insights which suggest a complete vision on the part of the author. It thus seems very likely that Margaret Laurence's expectations of the play will be fulfilled, namely that what is obscure to us 'may seem perfectly plain to the next generation of readers and play-goers'.[6]

Such comments will not impress the less dazzled reader who suspects that, far from embodying a supersubtle 'complete vision', the confusions here are caused by muddle and over-ambition on the part of the author. Such an inclination to take Soyinka on trust, seeking refuge in hints that the profoundly subtle unity underlying his work can only be guessed at by lesser mortals, is not infrequent in Soyinka criticism. Gerald Moore for instance shares the puzzlement of most readers as to the precise significance of Lazarus in *The Interpreters*. On the face of it he seems, with his resurrection

117

story and obscure rituals, to be a fraud or perhaps just mad. But some of the major characters take him and his claim to have risen from the dead oddly seriously, and he plays an increasingly central part in the action towards the end of the novel. What does Soyinka intend the reader to make of him? Moore dismisses the question thus:

> ... it may be that his claim to have risen from the dead is both literally bogus and imaginatively true. Or, to put it otherwise, it does not greatly matter whether it is true or not. What matters is that Lazarus now proves to be the figure who can unite Kola's canvas and express the divine Covenant of rainbow and multi-coloured boa, 'the vomit-streak of the heavenly serpent'.[7]

What does this mean? Indeed Kola does, as Moore says, place Lazarus in a central position in his picture of the Yoruba gods. But there must surely be some reason, symbolic or thematic, why this should be appropriate. Moore seems to suggest that Kola's painting is *in itself* a sufficient answer to the problems of Lazarus's thematic significance: or at least that Soyinka can see why Lazarus unites Kola's canvas even if we can't. Where Jones takes refuge in posterity Moore retreats into a formalistic approach which almost dispenses with anything so crude as actual meaning. Though these are perhaps extreme examples unfairly extracted from otherwise valuable critical works, they do represent a significant vein of Soyinka criticism.

The critic of the left (using the term in its widest sense) may offer a more mundane, political explanation of Soyinka's complexity and obscurity. Ngugi wa Thiong'o finds in Soyinka's idiosyncratic virtuosity a typically bourgeois self-indulgence, an assertion of the precious inviolability of his sensibility. According to this view Soyinka is a cynic: his adoption of ideals and causes is not an attempt to change the world, but merely to assert his personal superiority over it.

> The cynicism is hidden in the language (the author seems to revel in his own linguistic mastery) and in occasional flights into metaphysics. Soyinka's good man is the uncorrupted individual: his liberal human-ism leads him to admire an individual's lone act of courage, and thus often he ignores the creative struggle of the masses. The ordinary

people, workers and peasants, in his plays remain passive watchers on the shore or pitiful comedians on the road. [8]

J.P. O'Flinn sees Soyinka as fundamentally unconstructive, 'thumbing his nose' at authority rather than suggesting positive action. [9] By such accounts Soyinka appears as the prime representative in Nigeria of the intellectual wing of the underdeveloped bourgeoisie. While the cruder members of his class are indulging themselves in Western cars, stereo-systems and televisions, he indulges himself in Western decadent aestheticism or even those Western political ideologies in fashion with the middle-class intelligentsia. And like the European modernist he often resorts to a deliberate obscurity, designed to make his art the exclusive preserve of initiates. This is why the orthodox bourgeois critic, unwilling to betray ignorance or unworthiness, admiringly pronounces Soyinka's 'profundity' beyond elucidation. Like Solo, the narrator of Armah's novel *Why Are We So Blest?*, Soyinka has been seduced by the intricacies of Western art, philosophy and political thought, and ignores the urgent and simple needs of his own people. As Ngugi puts it, he plays no part in 'the creative struggle of the masses'.

Even Soyinka's various involvements in the practical politics of Nigeria could be cited in support of this view. His occasional eruptions into public affairs have frequently been criticised, even by his admirers, as flamboyant and melodramatic, rather than practical. While a student at University College, Ibadan, Soyinka founded a society called 'The Pirates', and, as Gerald Moore suggests, piracy, with all the swashbuckling individualism that word implies, has been his political element in later life. Moore relates the now legendary tale of how Soyinka supposedly forced his way into the Ibadan Radio Station (some say at gunpoint) during the crisis in the Western Region in November 1965, in order to substitute a tape announcing an Action Group election victory in place of the official tape announcing the actual, flagrantly rigged, NNDP victory.

Among those who believed the accusation [Moore says], many

admired Soyinka's courage; others felt that his concern with the dramatic gesture was likely to expose both him and others to dangers incommensurate with what it might achieve.[10]

His lonely stance during the early days of the civil war, his attempt to secure a UN arms ban and his conviction that Victor Banjo could lead a viable 'Third Force' in the conflict, can also be criticised as naive and impractical. Since the war he has resumed his 'piracy'. In April 1978, during the campus disturbances over the sudden reintroduction and increase of University fees, in which a number of students were killed, Soyinka resigned his position as 'special marshal' of Oyo State Road Safety Corps. Then, covering his car with placards accusing the police of brutality and demanding that the guilty be brought to justice, he drove round the official buildings of Ile-Ife.[11] Subsequently he 'disappeared' for a time, so that the police and their sympathisers could not find him.

The histrionics of Soyinka's public actions are paralleled in his writing, which may be felt to be similarly cavalier. Soyinka's personality looms large in his writing. He does not suffer fools gladly and is prepared to assert the special importance of his own experience in tones suggesting his superiority. For instance in the portentous 'Letter to Compatriots' at the beginning of *The Man Died* (1972):

> ... this book is *now*, and ... only such things should be left out which might imperil those on whom the true revolution within the country depends. My judgement alone must serve in such matters, and my experience which, it strikes me more and more, is unique among the fifty million people of my country.[12]

The peculiar hectic grandeur of Soyinka's self-dramatisation in the account of his imprisonment in *The Man Died* has been felt to ring somehow false. C. Tighe for instance feels that those poems in *A Shuttle in the Crypt* (1972) which were written actually at the time offer a more convincing picture of the chaos and misery of the real prison experience. *The Man Died* has, he says, been put through an 'ego-blender' after the event.[13] Certainly the overall tone of the book, despite its harrowing scenes, is strangely that of a triumphal progress of the author's spirit through adversity. And it is difficult to imagine another writer treating the experience in quite this heady, exhilarating way.

The central focus for any arbitration between the different critical views of Soyinka must fall on his expressed attitude towards commitment. Commitment has always been a theme in his work, whether on the level of religious self-sacrifice as in the case of Eman in *The Strong Breed* (1963), or of dedicated political violence as in the case of the Dentist in *Season of Anomy* (1973). When asked his views on the commitment of the writer, Soyinka placed the individual conscience at the centre of his complex answer.

> There are no binding laws of commitment . . . Each individual discovers sooner or later his own level and areas of commitment. If I had a choice in the matter I'd rather be a writer with no social commitment. That is by far the most comfortable form of creativity. For many years now I have lived with the knowledge that I could lose my liberty at any time. For reasons which I don't understand and cannot help, I am incapable of any peace of mind under certain social situations. There is nothing I can do about it, I can't change. Before one is a writer, I suppose one is a person.[14]

Genuine commitment is forced upon the individual by the pressures of living itself. It is not, as is often assumed, a simple matter of enlisting under a pre-existent banner. Commitment to specific social or political causes is a natural process, the consequence of a prior dedication on the individual's part to something more basic than political movements or ideologies—morality. Simply to 'join' a movement and give one's individuality up to superior direction is not commitment, but escapism. 'Morality, and therefore actions which come from a moral inspiration create the only "authentic being", they constitute the continuing personality of the individual and cannot be substituted by absolving palliatives.'[15] Morality is prior to any ideology; and ideology must not be substituted for it. The individual's existential choice cannot be evaded. During the civil war Soyinka considered it his duty to act in such a way as to 'demonstrate an ethical absolute even in the midst of the war'.[16] Whatever one may think of Soyinka's

121

'liberal humanism' it is difficult not to respect his rejection of the 'absolving palliatives' of blind faith and prejudice which so many mistake for commitment itself.

It is important also to realise that Soyinka is aware of the pitfalls of such individualism. His is not the 'soft' liberalism so scorned by the left, which turning in on itself and seeing everything in terms of conscience and consciousness, succumbs to the paralysis of self-doubt, and thus acquiesces in the injustice of the *status quo*. Action, he insists, is essential to real commitment. During the account in *The Man Died* of his conversation with Victor Banjo at the outbreak of war, contempt is expressed for the 'pseudo-socialist' intellectuals who fail to act at this time of crisis.

> 'You won't ever hear them,' I said. 'They are enjoying the anguish of having to decide between two evils.'
>
> Banjo said, 'The nation is not faced even with a choice of two evils. Whichever way this sort of war goes, the only results will be the entrenchment of the worst of both evils.
>
> 'The Soviets fought their Civil War gun in hand and political ideology in their heads. That was a whole half-century ago. But we thrust soldiers today into the field with just the slogan Kill-Yanmirin or Kill-Hausa. And for whose benefit? The damned bourgeois capitalists who have already begun to lap up the profits of a rising war industry. How do we get rid of the alliance of the capitalist adventurer and a bourgeois military after the war? Don't all these intellectuals know their history? Have they never heard of Spain?[17]

Banjo's analysis, clearly endorsed by Soyinka, is by no means that of a detached individualist, a self-indulgent sitter on the fence. Soyinka is, at this point at least, a 'hard' liberal, fully aware that the individual is not an inviolable and detached entity, and cannot help being involved in the political and economic system which has made his society what it is. Simply to remain inactive, is objectively to take sides. Hence Soyinka's practical attempts to find some way of avoiding the misconceived war into which Nigeria was sliding. Moreover Soyinka is also aware of the dangers for his writing of excessive individualism. All his work is explicitly or implicitly of the nature of a quest for 'authenticity', for his true self.

122

Such a quest invites self-indulgence. In Soyinka's own words: 'Narcissism begins when the writer fails to distinguish between self-exploration and self-manipulation.'[18] These are not the words of an unregenerate bourgeois individualist. And if in the course of our analyses we accuse Soyinka of indulging in self-manipulation in the guise of self-exploration, it is important to remember that in doing so we are using critical categories supplied by Soyinka himself.

It is finally crucial to any assessment of Soyinka's commitment to see his work in the context of the concrete realities of modern Nigeria. In Europe all kinds of different commitments, political, social or religious, are firmly embodied in precedent and tradition. For the contemporary Nigerian, as we saw in the first chapter, the effective expression of commitment in action may seem virtually impossible to achieve. In a society confused between tradition and modernity, with half-formed classes and atavistic rivalries (and, moreover, mass illiteracy) commitment can find few firm footholds. To what organisation, political party or definable 'movement' is the writer to commit him or herself? Where is it to be found? The element of personal histrionics in Soyinka's public actions is undeniable. But what other, more constructive, course can his critics suggest he should have taken during the First Republic and the Civil War? And the status he has created for himself since then, as a crusader on social and political issues, whose views are frequently quoted in the press as the voice of a nascent Nigerian 'public opinion', is surely by no means a negative one. In view of these considerations there must be a certain naivety in any straightforward condemnation of Soyinka for a failure of commitment. He may indeed be criticised for sharing the vices of his society and class. He does show an elitist arrogance at times, a desire to flaunt his cultural credentials. But on the other hand he is constantly examining his experience, attempting to understand himself and his society: to find a constructive role. And in this endeavour perhaps more of value emerges than from, say, the rather wooden, textbook demonstrations of neo-colonial forces to be found in such novels as Ngugi's

123

ideologically pure *Petals of Blood* (1977). It is perhaps in the very confusions and failures of Soyinka's work, as we shall see, that the most convincing picture of the full situation of his country is to be found.

## 'A Dance of the Forests' (1960)

*A Dance of the Forests* was first performed at Yaba Technical College, Lagos, in October 1960, the month in which Nigeria attained Independence. It won an *Encounter* magazine Independence Play Award, and as James Gibbs has pointed out[19] some aspects of the play suggest that it was completed in haste to meet the Independence deadline. Passages have been quarried from earlier, unpublished work, and in some cases, as Gibbs shows, speeches have been adapted virtually unchanged to contexts quite different from those for which they were originally written. It may be indeed that hasty composition is responsible for the unsatisfactory nature of some of the play's complexities. It is certainly an over-complicated and in some respects confusing work. Clearly it is intended as a symbolic comment on the prospects for Nigeria's future as a nation; and it seems equally clear that its message is broadly pessimistic. But its exact meaning, and the precise degree of its pessimism have been the subject of some critical discussion, focusing mainly on the masque with which the play ends.

*A Dance of the Forests* has none of the obvious topical specificity one might expect in a work written for so specific an event. Unlike the works of Achebe, or even Soyinka's own Jero plays, it deliberately transcends its Nigerian occasion, attempting a universal symbolic statement about all existence. Its comment on Nigeria's independence comes as part of a cyclic version of human history similar to that of Nietzsche, to whose work Soyinka had been introduced by his tutor at Leeds, George Wilson Knight. Dramatically speaking, this enactment of the constant cyclic repetition of human crime and suffering remains the strongest feature of the play. And the tantalising complexity with which the repetitive cycle is revealed in the lives of the three main human characters could be seen as a dramatic advantage rather than a defect, imparting as it does a sense of patterned inevitability to their destinies. The central play-within-a-play which takes all the characters back to the ancient court of the warrior-king Mata Kharibu, parallels each of the humans' modern crimes with an ancient equivalent committed in a previous life. In the present Demoke, the carver of trees, has murdered his apprentice out of jealousy of his superior climbing ability. In the past, as court poet to Mata Kharibu, he had pushed his novice from the roof of the palace where they had been sent to rescue the queen's pet canary. Rola, the present-day courtesan, has driven one of her lovers to murder the other and then commit suicide. In her previous incarnation as Mata Kharibu's queen she had caused a similar tragedy among the palace guards. Finally, and most inventively, Adenebi, the Council orator, has in the present accepted a bribe to pass a lorry, 'The Incinerator', suitable to carry seventy passengers, when it was only designed for forty, the result being that sixty-five people are killed when the overcrowded lorry catches fire. In his previous life as court historian to Mata Kharibu he had accepted a bribe from a slave dealer to pass a ricketty old ship sea-worthy with a capacity of sixty slaves. Through these parallels Soyinka suggests that history presents an inevitable repetitive cycle of evil. The moral problems of selfishness and corruption are not confined to any particular social or political context, but are universal and recurrent features of human nature.

The pessimism of Soyinka's view of humanity is brought into dramatic focus in the play-within-the-play by the confrontation between Mata Kharibu and his greatest warrior. This is the first treatment in Soyinka's work of one of his central concerns: the dissenting individual in conflict with the wickedness of constituted authority. The warrior refuses to take part in a war to regain the property of the queen whom Mata Kharibu has stolen from a neighbouring chieftain. He cannot see it, as the king does, as 'an affair of honour'. A complex debate develops between the warrior and various courtiers about the nature of individual integrity and the individual's duty to society. Soyinka's ability to embody abstract ideas and principles in tense and vividly realised theatrical action is amply illustrated in this scene. The Physician appeals to the verdict of posterity, arguing that 'Future generations will label you traitor'.[20] But the warrior is not concerned with opinion. Like Soyinka himself later in the civil war, he is asserting a 'moral absolute' which he must uphold, however futile his action may seem in practical terms, and however much it may be misunderstood.

PHYSICIAN: Unborn generations will . . .

WARRIOR: Unborn generations will be cannibals most worshipful Physician. Unborn generations will, as we have done, eat up one another. Perhaps you can devise a cure, you who know how to cure so many ills. I took up soldiering to defend my country, but those to whom I gave the power to command my life abuse my trust in them.[21]

It is the Historian (Adenebi) who produces the most crushing argument against the warrior's stubborn and heroic attachment to principle. He pounces on the warrior's faint, inconsistent hope that his action can inspire others in the future. In fact posterity will never hear of him, Adenebi says. Such protests as his against the general rule of immorality and war have remained unheard and unrecorded throughout history. (It is significant in this context that Soyinka gives the warrior no name.)

WARRIOR: But I am right. Perhaps I have started a new disease that catches quickly.

[Enter the Historian (Adenebi) with scrolls.]

HISTORIAN: Don't flatter yourself. Every blade of grass that has allowed its own contamination can be burnt out. This thing cannot last. It is unheard of. In a thousand years it will be unheard of. Nations live by strength; nothing else has meaning. You only throw your life away uselessly.[22]

The Historian's scrolls show no break in the repetitive consistency of history.

> War is the only consistency that past ages afford us.
> It is the legacy which new nations seek to perpetuate.
> Patriots are grateful for wars. Soldiers have never
> questioned bloodshed. The cause is always the
> accident your Majesty, and war is the Destiny. [23]

The 'new nations' referred to are clearly meant to include
Nigeria itself, and Soyinka's prophecy of war here was fulfilled only to soon. The Historian goes on to insist that
posterity values only violence and destruction. The glory of
Troy would have been quite forgotten if it had not been for
the carnage brought upon it by Helen (another stolen wife).
The warrior remains unmoved however, and although his preg-
nant wife and all the men under his command will be involved
in his ruin, refuses to give in. He is condemned to be castrated
and sold into slavery with his wife and followers. And to
underline the almost superhuman purity of his motives
Soyinka shows him refusing the queen's offer to save him, if
he will satisfy her lust and help her kill Mata Kharibu. There
is, it must be admitted, a hint of highfalutin artificiality
about this scene. It seems odd for instance (even in so symbolic a context) that the warrior and the courtiers should be
obsessed with something so abstract and intangible as posterity, when the security of the nation, the well-being of its
people and of the warrior's wife and soldiers would seem to
be of more immediate and pressing importance. But this is a
splendid piece of theatre nevertheless, and gives Soyinka's
rhetoric full scope.

In the main action of the play modern humanity, having
learnt nothing from history, once again rejects the warrior and
what he stands for. The gods respond to the human community's request for illustrious ancestors to attend their
'Gathering of the Tribes' (an obvious parallel with the Independence celebrations) by sending the warrior and his wife back
from the dead. The people, having expected someone more
like the glorious Mata Kharibu, are outraged and attempt to
drive the two ancestors away. So all the crimes of the past

have now been repeated; the cycle is unchanged. As Forest Head, the leader of the gods admits at the end of the play, it is impossible even for him to interfere and alter the pattern of human wickedness. All that can be hoped is that one or two souls will become 'aware', and then perhaps some break with the pattern may come.

> FOREST HEAD: [*more to himself*] Trouble me no further. The fooleries of beings whom I have fashioned closer to me weary and distress me. Yet I must persist, knowing that nothing is ever altered. My secret is my eternal burden—to pierce the encrustations of soul-deadening habit, and bare the mirror of original nakedness—knowing full well, it is all futility. Yet I must do this alone, and no more, since to intervene is to be guilty of contradiction, and yet to remain altogether unfelt is to make my long-rumoured ineffectuality complete; hoping that when I have tortured awareness from their souls, that perhaps, only perhaps, in new beginnings . .[24]

There are few signs in the play of such beginnings. There may be *some* sign however. Forest Head makes this speech at the climactic point in the masque which ends the play, while the artist, Demoke, is holding the 'half-child', uncertain on whom to bestow it. Forest Head's next words are: 'Aroni, does Demoke know the meaning of his act?' Perhaps we are meant to gather that Demoke is on the point of gaining the soul-awareness necessary for a new beginning? It is difficult to be certain of this, since it is at this point that the play becomes impenetrably obscure.

The various possible interpretations of Demoke's choice have been discussed by N. Wilkinson[25] and I do not propose to go into them in any detail. All critics agree that this scene is artistically and thematically confusing, though some are reluctant to admit that it is confused. Clearly the child of the Dead Woman, unborn at the time of her death in the slave ship, is meant to be symbolic; its ultimate fate indicates the destiny of society as a whole. But further than this it is impossible to go without meeting incoherence and contra-

diction. It is for instance unclear whether the (surely theatrically inevitable) return of the child to its mother is meant
to be a failure on Demoke's part: showing his inability to
break the repetitive cycle of suffering which it represents as
it 'circles yawning wombs', unable to break through into
life. Or whether perhaps it is a triumph: a final laying to
rest of the child and the evil it symbolises, allowing a fresh
start for humanity. Perhaps Demoke's action is an imitation
of the archetypal creative act of the patron god of artists,
Ogun, who first leaped into the abyss which had opened between gods and men. This creative leap is a central element in
Soyinka's personal myth of the artist. As he describes it in
his essay 'The Fourth Stage':

> The first actor—for he led the others—was Ogun, first suffering deity,
> first creative energy, the first challenger, and conqueror of transition.
> And his, the first art, was tragic art . . . The Yoruba metaphysics of
> accomodation and resolution could only come after the passage of
> the gods through the transitional gulf, after the demonic test of the
> self-will of Ogun the explorer-god in the creative cauldron of cos-
> mic powers.[26]

But if Demoke's action is an exertion of creative will why
does Eshuoro, a god of disorder, give 'a loud yell of triumph'
when the choice is made? Previously he had been 'furious' at
every step the child took towards its mother. Other similar
contradictions and obscurities abound.

As Wilkinson's article shows there has been much specula-
tion on the possible meanings of Demoke's choice and the
verdict which it implies on Nigeria's future. However any
search for the exact secret meaning which Soyinka has hidden
in his welter of ambiguous symbols seems doomed to failure.
The real critical question is *why* he has resorted to a welter
of ambiguous symbols to treat this subject. The answer is not
difficult to find. Soyinka is trapped between conflicting
impulses. On the one hand he seems pessimistically convinced
that the cycle of evil and suffering is unbreakable, and by
implication that Nigeria's Independence offers no real fresh
start. The villagers drive off the truly noble ancestors whom

129

the gods have sent to their festival. On the other hand he is passionately searching for some place within this pessimistic scheme for the creative act of the individual, particularly the artist, who, he would like to feel, can lead society forward. Soyinka cannot however find much genuine hope in the world as he perceives it, nor it must be admitted can he really expect the glorified creative artist to cut a very convincing figure as a saviour of his people, much as he would like to portray him as such. The result is that, adopting the complex subtlety of texture so prized in much modernist writing, he spins a rich and glossy coating of symbol and allegory around his central dilemma, just as an oyster secretes a pearl around its irritating stone of grit. Like much interesting writing *A Dance of the Forests* is an attempt by the author to reconcile himself to an unpalatable reality by investing it with rhetoric, symbol and virtuosity.

For all the perversity of its final scenes, this play could be seen as an authentic response to the social and political situation at the time of Nigeria's attainment of Independence. Its very confusion is meaningful. In one sense it represents an evasion of realities. Its extreme pessimism and grandly symbolic mode can be criticised as a bourgeois modernist escapism in the face of specific social problems. However it could also be argued that Soyinka's complex imaginative pattern, through its very evasions and uncertainties, captures the problems of his society with more human force than could any more direct and 'worked out' analysis. The Hungarian critic, Georg Lukács in his seminal work, *The Meaning of Contemporary Realism*,[27] distinguishes between art which arises as an organic, subjective response to the author's society, and that which sets out explicitly to analyse society. A Kafka presents his work 'without context' as it were, as an account of the, or a, human condition. While a Thomas Mann sets out to anatomise the social and political causes of the particular human condition of his own society. Lukács, as a Marxist, considers that there is no such thing as a universal 'human condition'. Nevertheless, the writing of a Kafka, he argues, may elucidate social conditions as effectively as that of a Mann. Crudely

130

speaking this is the distinction between literature as symptom and literature as diagnosis. The last section of *A Dance of the Forests* is very much a symptom of its confused society and time. And Soyinka's strength, like Kafka's, lies in his felt involvement in a confused and indeterminate situation, rather than in the lucid analysis of social or political particulars.

Throughout Soyinka's work, as we shall see, similar attempts are made to absorb political and social realities into an imaginative pattern, which will give them meaning and at the same time accommodate individual creativity. His views become grimmer and more explicitly political as he develops. Since the civil war, for instance, he has increasingly adopted the language of left-wing activisim. But the individual remains central throughout. The defiance of Mata Kharibu's warrior and the dilemma of Demoke recur in many forms in Soyinka's later work.

## 'The Interpreters' (1965)

Like *A Dance of the Forests* Soyinka's first novel is concerned with the linked themes of the relation of the individual to society and the role of the artist. But the context is less obviously symbolic than that of the play, closer to a recognisable, realistically portrayed modern Nigeria. On one level indeed the novel can be seen simply as Soyinka's *No Longer at Ease*, his treatment of the ubiquitous 'been-to' theme, relating the disappointments of the educated African returning from the West full of high ideals. (Soyinka characteristically complicates things by treating no fewer than five 'been-tos'.) Each of 'the new generation of interpreters',[28] as they are called at one point, has, like Achebe's Obi, recently returned from Europe with a determination to devote himself to the improvement of his society. And, Nigeria being what it is, each of them is disappointed. The resemblance to Achebe's novel does not go far however. Philosophical, religious and, above all, artistic themes occur in Soyinka's novel, unknown in Achebe's world. Several different interpretations of these

131

young men offer themselves. Indeed they are continually dis-
cussing different interpretations of themselves, and playing
with different possible commitments, in an attempt to
'interpret' themselves and their world. They are confused,
partly because of the social and political problems of their
environment, partly because of their immaturity (on one
level this is a novel about youth on the brink of adulthood),
and partly because of the intense aesthetic and intellectual
perfectionism which they all share. This last factor makes
them very distinctly Soyinkan personalities. It could even
be suggested that they are in fact all aspects of the same
character, projections of Soyinka himself, rather than rounded
novelistic creations. Their intensity, which dictates the often
contorted, ratiocinative style, deprives this work of the
'typicality' which makes Achebe's novels seem so central to
a practical understanding of modern Nigeria. But it gives it
far more complex resonances. Where Achebe's meticulous
and lucid analyses plot the impact of social and political
influences upon the individual, Soyinka conveys the tangled
density of individual experience, the texture of life in process. The reader is made to participate in the confusions of
the characters. Soyinka seems to have little concern for the
*stasis* which James Joyce felt essential for true art. This is a
decidedly *kinetic* novel.[29]

Broadly speaking the movement of the novel is from the
public world, in which failure and moral compromise seem
to be universal, into various private worlds, where the possibility of fulfilment is ambiguously projected. At first practical commitments seem possible to the three most thoroughly
treated of the 'interpreters'. Egbo is a promising young civil
servant and also heir to a traditional chieftaincy; Sekoni is a
brilliant engineer eager to develop the nation's potential for
the benefit of the people; Sagoe tries his hand at investigative
journalism. Each fails in his public role, because of the corruption of society and also, in Egbo's and Sagoe's cases,
because of what is termed their 'apostasy', their failure to
make the existential leap to total commitment, irrespective
of consequences. Each of them falls back into an individual,

132

personal commitment: in Egbo's case to religion, in Sekoni's to art, and in Sagoe's to marriage. The two other main 'interpreters', Bandele (a University lecturer) and Kola (an artist) remain more shadowy, emerging into prominence in the later part of the book, when the world of public affairs has been left behind. The novel's overall social theme is thus clear enough. It is in the treatment of the various individual commitments which replace the public ones that it becomes ambiguous and indeterminate.

Egbo seems to have the best opportunities for a successful public career. He works in the Foreign Office (although it must be said that there is little attempt to realise this aspect of his life in concrete terms), and he could if he chose play an important part in the traditional structure of society. The novel opens with Egbo hovering between the corrupt modern world which his civil service post represents and the world of the traditional past. He has taken his friends on a boat-trip up-river to visit his village, Osa, to which, as grandson of the chief, he could return and take up his place, with numerous wives and a great deal of political power. Indeed the 'Osa Descendants' Union' has been pressing him to return, 'bitten by the bug of "the enlightened ruler"',[30] and feeling that a young man with education would be best able to defend the village's interests within the modern political system of the nation. But although this role seems on the face of it essentially constructive and although this image of himself appeals to him, Egbo is reluctant to leave the familiar, urban, cosmopolitan life of the capital, despite its aimlessness and *ennui*. As the young men drift on the river, watching the village from a distance, Egbo with the exaggerated rhetoric of a self-dramatising young man, sets 'the warlord of the creeks against the dull grey filing cabinets of the Foreign Office'. His reaction is 'panic' at the necessity of making some kind of commitment.

> The spectre of generations rose now above him and Egbo found he would always shrink, although incessantly drawn to the pattern of the dead. And this, waiting near the end of the journey, hesitating on the brink, wincing as he admitted it—was it not exhumation of

133

a better forgotten past? Belatedly thinking, who am I to meddle? Who? Except—and this counted for much—that he knew and despised the age which sought to mutilate his beginnings.[31]

Egbo's choice is not a simple one between a glamorous past and an inglorious present. As in *The Lion and the Jewel*, but now in a more complex context, Soyinka shows himself sceptical in his evocation of traditional life. The old Oba, Egbo's grandfather, has his disreputable side; as 'warlord of the creeks' his power is a result of his control over smuggling routes and his wealth is gained by cheating the government of its taxes. Nevertheless Egbo feels the attraction of such a role, which can be made to seem full-blooded to an imagination bored with the spiritual squalor of the modern age. But Egbo remains irredeemably modern in outlook; the past cannot be real to him (nor perhaps to Soyinka himself) other than as an escapist image. Later Egbo expresses the wish that the past could remain sealed off as an escape-world from the pressures of the present.

'Is it so impossible to seal off the past and let it alone? Let it stay in its harmless anachronistic unit so we can dip into it at will and leave it without commitment, without impositions! A man needs that especially when the present, equally futile, distinguishes itself only by a particularly abject lack of courage.' [32]

He feels threatened by the demands made on him and sees his integrity in terms of resistance to commitment. His identity depends on the preservation of his precious neutrality.

It is while the characters discuss Egbo's dilemma, drifting on the river, that the term 'apostasy' is introduced, significantly perhaps, by Kola, the artist. Egbo seems to think that if they could only make the effort young men such as themselves could halt the collapse of their nation into mediocrity. Kola asks:

'Who will stop it? Your tired grandfather?'
'No. But we could.'
'But do we want to? Or try?'
'No. Too busy, although I've never discovered doing what. And that is what I constantly ask—doing what? Beyond propping up the

herald-men of the future, slaves in their hearts and blubber-men in fact doing what? Don't you ever feel that your whole life might be sheer creek-surface bearing the burdens of fools, a mere passage, a mere reflecting medium or occasional sheer mass controlled by ferments beyond you?'

Bandele shrugged. 'I don't work in the Civil Service.'

'But you acquiesce in the system. You exist in it. Lending pith to hollow reeds.'

'Is that why power attracts you?' Bandele asked.

'I merely want to be released from the creek-surface.'

'From apostasy.' Kola said.

'What's that?'

'What? Oh you mean apostate? An apostate, that's a face I cannot draw, even badly. You know, an absolute neutrality.'

One paddler felt in the water for movement. Anxiously said, 'The tide, it changes direction by late afternoon.'[33]

These words of the paddler gain symbolic significance when on the next page the tide does begin to turn. Egbo hesitates to give any order as to direction, and the boat is carried away from the village, back to the dissatisfactions of the modern world.

'All right, let's go.'

'Which way, man? You haven't said.'

Perhaps he had hoped they would simply move and take the burden of choice from him, but it was like Bandele to insist although motiveless. So, leaving it at that Egbo simply said,

'With the tide.'

Kola grinned. 'Like apostates?' [34]

Kola's question, we realise as the novel develops, hangs over not only Egbo, but also over the other main characters, who are all, with the exception of Sekoni, 'motiveless', neutral, uncommitted.

The first chapter ends with a succinct survey of the career of Sekoni, the only character to avoid 'apostasy'. He alone accepts the challenge of life and to the end refuses to acquiesce in the spiritual corruption which crushes him. Sekoni is a passionately religious man. He objects to Egbo's wish that the dead should not interfere with the living, asserting the

135

Yoruba idea of the oneness of all life, the co-existence of the dead, living and unborn in a 'dome of continuity'.[35] He is prepared to abandon selfhood and neutrality in commitment, and consequently it is he alone who actually comes near to achieving something in the world of action. Unlike Egbo he insists on being moved from the boring and comfortable office job where his talents are wasted. And when he is vindictively posted to a remote 'bush' region he grasps the opportunity to design and build an experimental power station. Unfortunately however the head of Sekoni's department can make nothing in bribes or 'dash' out of small economical power stations, however well-adapted to the needs of local communities they may be. So the design is condemned as dangerous by a bribed expatriate expert. And when Sekoni, in desperation, tries to fuel the station with his bare hands to prove that it will work safely, he is hauled off to a lunatic asylum. The political implications are clear and bleak. Sekoni's commitment dashes him to pieces against the *status quo*. His career is ruined, and he turns his thwarted creativity to sculpture, producing a masterpiece, 'The Wrestler'. He dies shortly afterwards in a car crash.

The other 'interpreters' are less committed and by taking fewer risks ensure for themselves an ignoble and dissatisfied survival. Sagoe, whose experiences are recounted next, represents a typical case. Much of the explicit social satire of the novel is conveyed through this, the most down-to-earth of the 'interpreters'. His interview for an appointment as journalist with the ironically named *Independent Viewpoint* gives Soyinka many opportunities for broad, Dickensian caricature. Throughout his encounters with the grotesque Chief Winsala and Sir Derinola, Sagoe preserves an illusion of detachment from their corruption through his mock-philosophy of 'Voidancy': exorcising his disgust at moral filth by elevating the excretion of physical filth to the status of a fine art. The fact that he cannot remain aloof and that his integrity is in reality totally compromised, is brought home to him when he attempts to exercise his talents usefully in exposing the corruption which led to the condemnation of his friend Sekoni's

power station. He is surprised to learn that, although Sir
Derinola, the chairman of the paper's board, is delighted with
his work on the story, it is not to be printed. The editor
explains:

> 'Shut your mouth, I shut mine. Plain and simple. You have got
> the chairman out of some nasty jam.'
> 'I have *what*?'
> 'It goes on all the time. You see, it is part of the mutual protec-
> tion. Before we publish any revelation like that, it must go to our
> lawyers. And he in turn consults with the Chairman. It is out of our
> hands.'
> 'Go on. I am anxious to learn.'
> 'Well he lets the other side know what he has got on them. If
> they decide they can weather it, they say go ahead. If not, they say,
> Well as a matter of fact we have been collecting certain things about
> Such-and-such a person on your side, and they send a copy along.
> Well I have a pretty good idea what Sir Derin had got himself into,
> but anyway your copy came in the nick of time. They have done a
> swap of silences.'
> 'And what about my friend?'
> Nwabuzor shrugged as much as to say, What can I do?[36]

The appalling irony of the affair is that, while Sagoe thought
that he was working for the vindication of his friend and to
expose corruption, he has in fact merely been helping the corrupt Derinola to escape exposure. His work has had no other
effect than to preserve the *status quo*. He has been carried
'with the tide'. And there is no escape since all the newspapers
work within the same system, and so none of them will take
Sagoe's story. Unlike Sekoni, Sagoe accepts defeat and adapts to
it. He takes refuge in an inert and cynical fatalism, or indulges
in more and more extravagantly escapist flights of 'Voidancy'.

> 'Don't mind me Mathias,' [he says to the office boy.] 'I know I
> am feeling sorry for myself, and over nothing. People like Sekoni end
> up on the pyre anyway, but damn it, I didn't have to help them build
> the faggots.'
> Mathias drained his bottle. 'Na so life be oga.'
> 'Silence, Mathias. Silence. I have known all kinds of silence, but
> it's time to learn some more.'[37]

137

After their various failures the characters begin to give up their ambition to 'convert the world'[38] and turn to more personal and individual roads to fulfilment. As Shatto Arthur Gakwandi says:

> At the beginning of the novel they are talking in terms of changing the social reality of their country. At the end they have given this up and only talk in terms of expressing their frustration through art, just as Sekoni, who tried hard to put his ideas into practice, was defeated by the system and finally turned to sculpture. Art becomes a means of expressing the ugliness of the reality which the individual cannot change.[39]

Perhaps Gakwandi's reference to art requires some expansion. Although art seems to offer the most authentic consolation, there are several others in the novel. Egbo turns to religious mysticism, Sagoe to his fantastic 'philosophy' and eventually to marriage, and only for Sekoni and Kola does 'art' proper take a central place. Exactly what the 'interpreters' turn to is perhaps less important however than the fact that all their ways to fulfilment (except perhaps Sagoe's marriage) assert an essential detachment from the rest of societ , an elitist superiority over it. It is of the greatest importance in this respect that the character who does not hold himself aloof, who commits himself most selflessly to socially useful action, Sekoni, achieves the truest self-expression in art. The apostasy of all the other characters prevents them from achieving not only effective practical action, but also satisfying spiritual self-expression. Kola himself acknowledges the weakness of his painting of the Yoruba gods, while the energy of the others seems to express itself not in primary creativity, but most often in the assertion of good taste, which at least elevates them above their environment if it does nothing else. One of the most successful minor strands in the novel is its contemptuous satire on philistinism—the director at Sagoe's interview for instance, with his delicate china:

> The Director had picked up the set in the tenth economic mission to American China; he donated it to the Board remarking, 'You know, Shanghai Chek has exactly this kind of cup and saucer.'[40]

138

Then there is Professor Oguazor with his plastic fruit and his wife 'Ceroline', who responds to Kola's art by 'testing the paint to see if it came off'.[41] As the novel draws to its close the 'interpreters' seem more and more isolated and at bay, defending their precious individualistic sensibilities against this hostile world. A sense of disappointment and anticlimax pervades the novel.

There is an ambiguity in the later part of the novel however which is the source of real weaknesses. At times it seems that Soyinka himself is attempting a similar individualistic transcendence of society to that of his characters. He seems to want to convince himself and his readers that some at least of the 'interpreters'' private escape worlds are more than that: are indeed roads to true fulfilment rather than the consolations forced on them by failure. Egbo is the key case here. Right from the start there is a mixture of levels in his portrayal: a realistic social level and a mythic, religious level. At first this complex blend of realism and symbol imparts depth and richness to his characterisation. As an orphan with a European education and descended from the traditional rulers of his village, his difficult, distant, oversensitive personality seems perfectly realistic. Also on the level of the social theme his refined sensibility is clearly an excellent register of the alienation from society which afflicts all the 'interpreters'. On the other hand there are symbolic elements in his portrayal which give him something of the mystery and glamour of a folk-tale hero. He is a handsome aristocrat with a touch of the Byronic about him. He is constantly associated with the god of creativity and war, Ogun, and at one point seems to commune with and challenge the gods in a mystical trance beside the river Ogun. As a baby he was saved by a miracle from the accident in which both his parents were drowned (at the very spot where the boat is drifting at the beginning of the novel). The element of water seems to define his character. He frequently sees his life in terms of drifting or allowing himself to be carried away by outside forces. His destiny he says is 'a choice of drowning'.[42] Sometimes the references to water and drifting are used as images for a literal social alienation.

139

At other times Egbo seems to exist on a non-literal level of symbol and mysticism. Is he a real-life illustration of the alienation of creative youth in modern Nigeria, or is he a fated being, following or challenging the destiny assigned to him by the gods? At different points Soyinka seems to imply that he is both. The question is complicated by the fact that Egbo (with perhaps a pun on 'ego') is clearly closely related to Soyinka himself, who was born on the banks of the river Ogun (at Abeokuta), and who as an artist associates himself with Ogun. Perhaps Egbo's mysterious glamour is mere flattering self-projection on the author's part. Certainly as the novel develops such symbolic elements increasingly conflict with the implications of the social and political theme. Mythical or transcendental explanations seem to be suggested for attitudes and states of mind which have already been accounted for realistically, in terms of socially determined influences. Moreover Soyinka's treatment of this aspect of Egbo begins to show an awkwardness and failure of definition. The conversation with the girl student whom he takes to the place of his mystical experience is stilted and pretentious (and also shows gross male chauvinism).

> Egbo stopped, unable to contain his delight. 'You certainly show spirit. In fact, I think you are a very delightful person. Most students I know are not.' . . .
>
> 'You like Omar Khayam?' [she asks.]
> 'I know and like but that one tetrastich—that's the name, isn't it?'
> 'But what do you mean, enigmatic?'
> 'If I knew that I wouldn't call you that, would I?' . . .
>
> 'If you are not afraid and can stay until the shadows lengthen, you will see it darken behind the pair [of statues] giving greater depth within the alcove.' [43]

And the description of the mystical experience itself is afflicted by emotional vagueness and a hollow abstraction of vocabulary.

> He had loved darkness, silent stagnation. But not this roar of deadness and the blindness of its path. Overslept in caverns in the dark dwellings of an avenging God? By whose remote design? Whose Siren

stole the touch of teething breezes!

Till he grew bold with fear, and angry, truly angry. What mean trick was this? Whose was the dark-sheltered laughter spying on his plight! And his anger mounted, seeing only the blackmail of fear.

If this be sin?—and he knew that his weakening had come from this so he ended it. If this be sin—so—let come the wages, Death!

And he lay back on the rocks, and slept.

And morning came . . .[44]

The Egbo of this passage seems to have ascended into a realm of inchoate mystical melodrama, plausible enough perhaps as the adolescent effusion of a hypersensitive and egotistical young man. But the author seems to want the reader to take it more seriously than this. He seems to be cooperating, with some enthusiasm even, in Egbo's self-indulgent 'ego-trip', as also in his sexual adventure with the 'enigmatic' student.

A similar hollowness of treatment affects Lazarus, the charismatic resurrectionist preacher. In the context of the novel's social theme it is possible to give Lazarus a perfectly straightforward interpretation. This is what Gakwandi does. He attacks those critics who feel that Lazarus does not fit into the artistic design of the book, offering his own lucid and rational interpretation.

> These critics have failed to see that Lazarus is one of the interpreters. His bizarre prophetism is his own means of escaping from both the moral emptiness of his society and his social limitations. Seen objectively, his behaviour is no more eccentric than Sagoe's voidancy, Egbo's mysticism or Sekoni's 'dome of continuity'. All these characters have been driven by frustrated spiritual yearnings into eccentric modes of self-expression.[45]

Such a version, placing Lazarus and his religion firmly within the social theme would indeed seem to make the best and most coherent sense in the context of the novel as a whole. But many readers will wonder whether Soyink's view of Lazarus (or of Egbo) is quite as 'objective' as Gakwandi's. If the author's intention is that described by Gakwandi why does he take up so much space surrounding Lazarus with portentous and intricate symbolic paraphernalia? In relation to Kola's picture, for example. First of all Kola intends to paint Noah,

141

Lazarus's convert, as Christ; then he changes his mind and decides to paint him as Esumare, the rainbow, symbol of the covenant between gods and men (his name seems to prompt this). But finally Kola realises his mistake and substitutes Lazarus himself for Noah. What is all this complicated symbolic semaphore supposed to tell us? That the covenant between gods and men is an illusion perhaps, since Lazarus is a fraud? (What in that case would have been the significance of Noah as Esumare?) One problem is that Kola's painting, symbolically central though it is, is never sufficiently described or explained for one to work out its full structure or significance. Altogether there are too many hints of symbolic depths in the treatment of Lazarus, and not enough actual meaning to be gleaned from them. What for instance is the significance of the scene which Egbo witnesses at night by the flooded church, when Noah runs off from an enigmatic ritual ordeal to which Lazarus invites him, floating across a neck of water between paraffin flares? Is it simply another (rather ponderous) symbol of apostasy? If it is merely part of Lazarus's 'eccentric' mumbo-jumbo, as Gakwandi's version would suggest, why is Egbo (and clearly also the author) so earnestly fascinated by it and why is it described in such great detail?[46]

The explanation of these problems must lie in a similar equivocation on Soyinka's part to that we saw in *A Dance of the Forests*. On the one hand Soyinka's realistic analysis of society leaves little hope that his characters can reach any kind of satisfying fulfilment. On the other hand as a liberal individualist Soyinka would dearly like to assert that fulfilment can be achieved solely within the individual—that there are spiritual levels of experience beyond the reach of social forces. Hence his preoccupation with mysticism and myth. It must be admitted however that the most effective parts of the book remain those which treat social and political themes realistically. It is perhaps a tribute to the authenticity of Soyinka's art that the novel's more arcane and spiritually elitist elements fail to convince. The final effect of *The Interpreters* is, like that of Sekoni's 'Wrestler', one of baffled and thwarted creative energy.

## 'Season of Anomy' (1973)

The civil war marks a turning-point in Soyinka's career; but one that is more apparent than real. After his release from internment in 1969 his work is more bitter and more explicit in its treatment of political issues. But his basic themes and attitudes remain the same, and the same critical problems recur. It would be convenient to be able to see the war as purging Soyinka's self-indulgent egotism and rousing him to 'mature' commitment. But this would not be accurate. A key passage in *The Man Died* (1972) indicates the actual ambiguities of his response to this public and personal crisis. He begins quite egocentrically, finding in the war a fulfilment of the prophecies of this earlier work and an illustration of his cyclic view of history.

> Again and again I recognize this territory of existence. I know that I have come to this point of the cycle more than once, and now the memories are so acute that I wonder if it has not been truly a mere prophetic expectation of it all, in the waiting upon it in captive attendance, wondering merely, when?[47]

On the public level, his forecast of the return of the evil of past generations has been vindicated, and on the personal level (it is hinted) he, Soyinka, is now in real life acting out the role of the warrior in *A Dance of the Forests* or Eman in *The Strong Breed*. He is the fated sacrifice, the tragic victim, caught in the predestined cycle. However he is not fully comfortable with this tragic self-projection, and the rest of the passage goes on to analyse and question it.

> A private quest? Stuff for the tragic stage and the ritual rounds of Passion? A brave quest that diverges from, with never a backward glance at history's tramp of feet along the communal road? Is this then the long-threatened moment for jettisoning, for instance, notions of individual responsibility and the struggle it imposes? Must I now reject Kant? Karl Jaspers? 'However minute a quantity the individual may be in the factors that make up history, he is a factor.' Must I now say to him, yes a dead factor?[48]

143

A loss of self in glad identification with a larger communal existence, such as is advocated by Ngugi, is quite alien to Soyinka. The phrase 'history's tramp of feet along the communal road' rings not with the 'scientific' faith of the Marxist in the 'laws' of historical development, but with the despair of the Nietzschean pessimist at the barren cycles of history. This is the stuff of tragic heroism: the pointless and thus magnificent assertion of human values in an indifferent universe. Adversity is to be embraced, not for any practical good it may bring, but as necessary to the individual's attainment of 'authenticity'. Soyinka quotes 'Man can only grasp his authentic being through confrontation with the vicissitudes of life.' But at this point the argument turns upon itself. Such glorification of the tragic individual is too crudely self-regarding, and must be rejected.

> I have quarrelled too often even with the ego-centred interpretations to which the existentialist self gives rise. Any faith that places the *conscious* quest for the inner self as goal, for which the context of forces are mere battle aids is ultimately destructive of the social potential of that self. Except as a source of strength and vision keep inner self out of all expectation, let it remain unconscious beneficiary from experience. Suspect all conscious search for the self's authentic being; this is favourite fodder for the enervating tragic Muse.

So, socially constructive action must take precedence over self-dramatising introspection, and the self will ultimately be the better off for being effaced. Tragedy, with its concentration on the isolated individual, is to be rejected as an enervating indulgence. At this point Soyinka seems to be moving towards a more activist political position, if in his own distinctive way. The *status quo*, he says, uses the safety-valve of tragedy to keep the individual quiescent, and prevent social change.

> Against all questioning and change, against concrete redress of the causative factors of any crisis, society protects itself by this diversion of regenerative energies into spiritual in-locked egotism. To ensure that there is no reassertion of will the poetic snare of tragic loftiness is spread before him . . .[49]

For the artist then, tragic self-projection is a trap. So, although Soyinka does not advocate the orthodox subordination of self to 'the cause', he is nevertheless an enemy to the barren individualistic self-regard which, by containing human creative energy, prevents social regeneration.

Soyinka's method of argument is very slippery and at times elusive. Even when what he is saying is quite straightforward the style invests it with a dense complexity. One may suspect him of too great an involvement in the individual peculiarities of his own personality, even as he rejects egotism. Is it self-exploration or self-manipulation that we are witnessing in this passage? He wishes to reject his own tendency towards self-indulgence, but is unwilling to rush from the extreme of bourgeois individualism into the opposite extreme of barren communalism or a vulgar Marxist undervaluing of the individual. So he hovers, arguing earnestly with himself, in an ill-defined middle-ground which seems to contain little more than his own contorted self-doubt. He is himself aware of a certain potential for absurdity in his convoluted self-questionings. The typically off-beat image 'I try to feed some muscularity into the marshmallow of sensations',[50] is masterly in its combination of on the one hand a genuine expression of an inchoate state of consciousness, and on the other a suggestion of self-mockery. It is this ability to capture the density of thought in process, with all its unpredictable refocusings and shifts of mood, which gives Soyinka's style in passages like this its exasperating yet exhilarating fascination. As his questionings become more knotty and involved he begins to seek relief in offhandedness. At first the rhetoric mounts:

> I seek only the combative voices and I hunt them down from remotest antiquity to the latest incidental re-encounters on casual forums. 'Tragedy is merely a way of retrieving human unhappiness, of subsuming it and thus of justifying it in the form of necessity, wisdom or purification. The rejection of this process and the search for the technical means of avoiding the insidious trap it lays is a necessary undertaking today.'[51]

Then the strain breaks in sudden irritability.

145

When? Where? I neither remember nor care. I recall only that I once made a note of it to use in what a student called my special anti-literature seminars.

A contemptuous outburst follows which seems to reassert Soyinka's personal superiority over the ignorant multitude who accept the *status quo*. Then it is undercut at the last moment by an admission of common humanity.

But the words hammer strident opposition to the waves of negations that engulf me, to the mob hatred that I distinctly hear even in this barred wilderness. It nerves me to mutter—Brainwashed, gullible fools, many-headed multitudes, why should your voices raised in ignorance affect my peace?
But they do. I cannot deny it.

The sense of strain, even of desperation, in this passage, is characteristic of much of Soyinka's later work. It is a strain generated by conflicting philosophies (and conflicting moods) jostling against each other, presenting a kaleidoscope of shifting explanations of the world. Soyinka it seems can never be certain, even of his own thought-processes. 'Do I or do I not recognize the trap'[52] of tragic existentialism, he asks himself. It is a characteristic question and central to all his work. The reader's answer to it will depend on how positively he or she responds to Soyinka's idiosyncratic thought-processes. The unsympathetic reader will convict him of continuous and gross elitist self-importance—even his parading of self-doubt being merely another kind of egotism. Others will find in him a fascinating and genuine embodiment of the dilemmas of contemporary humanity, notable for its refusal to escape into the consoling simplifications offered by ideologists from all sides. Perhaps (if such a compromise is possible!) a true assessment of Soyinka would lie somewhere between these two versions.

A particularly complex instance of this problem is presented by Soyinka's second novel. *Season of Anomy* embodies the later Soyinka's most explicit position with regard to politics and the individual's—more particularly the artist's—relation to public affairs. The pessimistic retreat into the private

146

self found in *The Interpreters* has been superseded by an energetic attempt to realise his 'social potential', to forge a practical rationale for revolutionary action. This novel is the nearest thing in Nigerian fiction to the kind of politically committed literature of the left represented elsewhere in Africa by Sembene Ousmane's *Les Bouts de Bois de Dieu* (1960) and Ngugi wa Thiong'o's *Petals of Blood* (1977). In its own Soyinkan way it seems to be attempting to break through to Fanon's third phase of colonial and post-colonial writing. According to Fanon, after the second phase, which as we have seen is marked by nostalgic evocations of traditional life and the 'distress and difficulty' of the divided consciousness, a 'fighting' phase ensues.

> ... the native, after having tried to lose himself in the people and with the people, will on the contrary shake the people ... he turns himself into an awakener of the people; hence comes a fighting literature, a revolutionary literature, and a national literature.[53]

Soyinka's complex novel is, it must be admitted, nothing like the kind of propagandist 'national literature' which Fanon envisages. Fanon, thinking primarily in terms of the Algeria of his day and moreover possessing little understanding of art, sees literature as an educative instrument, used by the activist intellectual to raise the consciousness of the illiterate and oppressed peasantry. Fanon quotes in illustration an extraordinarily dreary anti-colonial poem by Keita Fodeba, praising its 'unquestioned pedagogic value'.[54] Soyinka's artistic world is in a different dimension from this kind of thing. Nor does Soyinka take the more complex but still firmly ideological line of an Ngugi or a Sembène, focusing on proletarian or peasant characters who compose a multiple 'communal' protagonist. His attention is still engrossed by the sensitive consciousness of the individual intellectual, and it is through such a consciousness—that of Ofeyi—that most of the action is viewed. However, the action *is* viewed with a sense of the urgent and pressing need for revolutionary action new to Soyinka's work. In this sense it is a 'fighting' book, a call to arms.

147

If we leave aside for the moment the novel's layers of symbol and allegory, it can be seen to offer a lucid analysis of post-colonial politics with a clear, if never explicitly stated, application to the case of Nigeria. The setting of the novel is closely based on the Nigeria of summer 1966, although there is some free adaptation. Soyinka's main political theme in the first chapters is the association between the military government and the commercial interests of the bourgeois class, embodied in 'the Cartel'. The Cartel, we are told, had 'identified itself with the new power from the barrel'.[55] And when Ofeyi, a disaffected promotions officer for the Cartel begins a campaign to undermine it by hiding ironies and counter-propaganda in the advertisements which he devises, it is significantly a government 'trouble-shooter' who is sent to put him in his place. Soyinka's treatment indicates that the real sources of tension within society are not the apparent ones of regionalism and atavism. These are merely tools in the hands of class interests. In Soyinka's version the outbreak of tribalism in the Northern massacres is in fact a deliberately orchestrated diversionary tactic, used by the alliance of military government and bourgeoisie for their own material ends. The Cartel is a socio-economic ruling-class or 'establishment' in the modern sense, itself quite free from the traditional motives which it so cynically manipulates. The champagne party which the Western Governor, Batoki, gives for the Northern traditional leader, the Zaki Amuri, 'confirmed his own loyalty to a sodality that transcended mere regionalism. The only party that truly transcends local boundaries'.[56] Material interest is the true motive behind apparently atavistic violence. The Cartel, intent on destroying the men of Aiyéró, who symbolise—on this level of the novel at least—progressive political opposition, is compelled to resort to wider bloodshed:

> They were after the men of Aiyéró everywhere. But they have to disguise it by unleashing death on a far wider scale.[57]

The application to the Nigerian situation is obvious. In order to destroy the more politically active and aware elements in society, Soyinka is implying, the establishment directed hatred against all Ibos, from among whom many such activists came. Aiyéró symbolises a new working-class awareness working against the imposition by the Cartel of a new version of the old colonial slavery.

> The goals were clear enough, the dream a new concept of labouring hands across artificial frontiers, the concrete, affective presence of Aiyéró throughout the land, undermining the Cartel's superstructure of robbery, indignities and murder, ending the new phase of slavery.[58]

The political mission of the revolutionary 'cadres' of Aiyéró is made quite explicit. They are raising the consciousness of the working masses, a process which can be seen in the building of the new dam at Shage, symbolically situated on the border between North and South.

> New projects like the Shage Dam meant that we could start with newly created working communities. New affinities, working-class kinships as opposed to the tribal. We killed the atavistic instinct once for all in new ventures like Shage.[59]

The unscrupulous means by which the established power distorts this struggle to its own ends is shown, with something of the diagrammatic quality of 'agit-prop' in Chapter VIII, in the trial before the Zaki of a Northern sympathiser with Aiyéró. The man is threatened and bullied, his Moslem religion is invoked (since the Zaki is a religious as well as a secular leader), his suspicions of the infidel Southerners is played upon, and his ignorance and illiteracy are used against him when he is told that the petition for higher pay which he has signed has in fact given away his land. His more enlightened brother-in-law, who is accused of tricking him into this self-dispossession, cannot refute the charge since he is in the Zaki's gaol. There is a certain element of caricature in this scene, and Soyinka's treatment of his political theme relies heavily on such simplifications of the Nigerian reality for its effect. Clearly the people and the events of the novel are not identical with those of Nigeria, although there are essential and extensive parallels. The licence of fiction allows Soyinka to omit inessential detail and emphasise hidden tendencies,

149

tendencies not fully visible, or perhaps not even fully formed, within real-life Nigeria. His analysis thus has far more forcefulness than could a more literal documentary. The portrayal of the Cartel and of Aiyéró illustrate this. It would be difficult to identify any single unified organisation in Nigeria which would correspond with the Cartel of the novel, based as it is on a single industry (cocoa) and working so concertedly throughout the nation for specific ends. Nor in real life is there yet any organised movement for social change of the kind and on the scale of Aiyéró. What Soyinka has done is to isolate and project certain real and crucial elements within Nigerian society, using the greater clarity and imaginative coherence of art in order to draw out their essential political implications.

On one level then *Season of Anomy* can be seen as a political allegory of the situation in Nigeria at the time of the first pogroms. Woven into this is a second political theme—a more developed and complex treatment of the question of individual commitment familiar from his earlier works. Ofeyi's liberalism is viewed with new potential ironies, and in his discussions with the Dentist, a dedicated, politically motivated assassin, he seems to be moving away from humane liberalism towards an acceptance of the necessity for violence to achieve political progress. Ofeyi remains however, in spite of everything, true to type: very much the subtle, scrupulous, humane sensibility. At times he suggests interpretations of political events of a quite apolitical kind, in terms of human nature, climate or metaphysical 'evil'. Confronted in the North with a broken-down cripple he reflects on the

> sheer cussedness of the Cross-river environment, its frequent epidemics, blindness inflicting plagues, spinal infections and mind-drugging flies. Ofeyi wondered briefly, confronted by this half-human apparition, was the blood-lust that seized upon the populace just another legacy of climate? Another deformity like the effects of meningitis or the blood-poisoning of the tse-tse fly? A diminished responsibility created by a virus in the air, flooding the victims with a need to degrade more fortunate humanity in an image of their own pain and desecration? Or was there a truly metaphysic condition called evil,

present in epidemic proportions, that made them so open to the manipulations of coldly unscrupulous men? There had to be a cause beyond mere differences in culture, beyond material envy . . .[60]

This passage, occuring very near the end of the book, suggests that Ofeyi never succumbs to the single-mindedly ideological view of political events of the Dentist. There is a problem here however, which causes difficulty throughout the novel, in assessing Soyinka's attitude towards Ofeyi. How much irony is there? It is perhaps significant that the cripple who is the occasion of these reflections is later revealed to be a man of courage and heroism. Is this meant to reflect on Ofeyi's judgement? Similarly, the phrase 'wondered briefly' is perhaps meant to be a shade apologetic, implying an aberration on Ofeyi's part. As was the case with Egbo, it is difficult to be certain about such possible ironies in the case of a character who is so clearly an authorial self-projection.

Certainly the liberal individualism which Ofeyi represents is shown to be very hard pressed by the opposing ideology of the Dentist. On many occasions Ofeyi seems to have no defence against the Dentist's arguments. His reluctance to contemplate violence against the members of the Cartel who are known to him on a personal level as pathetic or even sympathetic people, is for instance witheringly derided by the Dentist. This is mere sentimentality, he claims, reminding Ofeyi of the crimes perpetrated by their class.

'I still insist' the Dentist commented, 'self-defence is not simply waiting until a lunatic attacks you with a hatchet. When you have watched his attack on a man up the road, you don't wait any longer. But you see, you rationalists have given birth to a monster child by pretending that the lunatic can be reasoned with. That is why our people die.'[61]

In an attempt to soften the Dentist's ideological ruthlessness by appealing to his personal, human responses Ofeyi takes him to visit Batoki, with whose daughter he is acquainted. The scene of shabby domestic squabbling which Ofeyi witnesses, as the mother and daughter fight for the favour of the father, is one of the most brilliant in the book, and is an excellent

151

illustration of the way power and wealth corrupt even the private lives of their possessors. Ofeyi expresses a typical liberal response as he drives away with the Dentist.

> 'I wish you had witnessed that shabby family scene . . . no, don't waste your time on Batoki. He is not worth killing.'
> The Dentist's face hardened and he turned a faintly supercilious glance on Ofeyi. 'Shall I put that another way for you? What about this: the family is suffering already, don't bring any more misery upon them. Or: their opulence and self-indulgence has brought them no happiness, so let them extort and mutilate those who resist to their heart's content . . . [62]

There seems little doubt that the Dentist wins the argument here and has the endorsement of the author. And increasing exposure to the horrors perpetrated by the Cartel forces Ofeyi more and more to agree with him.

> It seemed a sacrilege, with memories such as this [a murdered woman and her child], to admit to death-wish as contained in a refusal to accept the burden of decision when that decision could—if the Dentist was right—end all repetition of such images as this. The truth was too bare for self-deceit, the call for urgent action too strident for any evasion. The Dentist appeared to have set his course on the only possible sanity, leaving the rest slaves to rationalist or emotive fantasies. [63]

Even here however Ofeyi does not actually commit himself. '*If* the Dentist was right' he says. Moreover the murders he has just witnessed have already been reduced from objective reality to a function of his introspective consciousness: 'with *memories* such as this', 'such *images* as this'. On the Dentist's terms, it seems, Ofeyi is incurable. And so perhaps is Soyinka.

The debate between Ofeyi and the Dentist is at the centre of the novel's political theme. Unfortunately however the terms within which it is conducted show an evasiveness on the author's part which may lead the reader to doubt whether the full implications of the issue have really been canvassed. We have already mentioned the difficulty of gauging the degree of Soyinka's irony in relation to Ofeyi. Different but related doubts attach to the Dentist's credentials. It seems unfortunate for instance that we do not see this dedicated assassin actually killing anybody. An actual murder of a character with whom the reader has become acquainted (such as Batoki) would surely be the best way of dramatising the debate between revolutionary violence and personal scruple. But Soyinka avoids this, choosing instead to stress the Dentist's glamour, his sinister, cloak-and-dagger 'loyal squad of thugs' and the romantic appeal of his 'notorious legend'.[64] Cogent and forceful though his arguments may be therefore, the Dentist is in dramatic terms a rather dubious representative of the dedicated revolutionary assassin. He remains quite un-implicated in the real violence actually portrayed in the novel, all of which is perpetrated by or on behalf of the Cartel. During their 'tour' of the devastation both Ofeyi and the Dentist become oddly removed from reality. They take on something of the charmed inviolability of adventure-story heroes, an impression reinforced by the (admittedly dramatically effec-tive) placing of their visit to Batoki in Chapter X, as a paren-thesis, quite outside the narrative sequence of Ofeyi's journey to the North. It is unfortunate again for the Dentist's imagina-tive and ideological coherence that Ofeyi never seriously questions the rationale behind his plan of selective assassina-tion. Ofeyi's attack on the Dentist (or rather defence of him-self) is purely in terms of the moral distastefulness of killing fellow human beings. But surely a more cogent questioning would throw doubt on the very claim to political effective-ness of the Dentist's policy. It is at least not self-evident that structural injustices within a complex social system can be cured by killing those individuals who happen to head this system at any given moment. Although Ofeyi is uncertain 'if the Dentist was right', this criticism from a political rather than a 'humane liberal' standpoint is not articulated in the novel. Ofeyi simply accepts that if he is to abandon his liberal scruples then the Dentist offers *the* alternative. The wider political simipifications of the novel's structure help to give a spurious plausibility to this view. The unifying of all the military and bourgeois factions of real-life Nigeria into one symbolic organisation—'the Cartel'—effective though it may

153

be in some ways, tends to make the Dentist's solution through assassination seem more feasible than it could possibly be in reality. It suggests a very simple relation between the powerful individual and the wider social reality. We are just meant to accept that the two heads of the Cartel who are portrayed in any detail, Batoki and the Zaki Amuri, are somehow instigators and prime movers of the system, which would collapse without them. Is there not an undue personalisation of the true nature of politics and of society itself here? The failure of the *coup* of January 1966, carried out very much on the Dentist's principles, shows that in real life the assassination of individuals solves few (if it does solve some) problems.

Most damaging of all, however, to the Dentist's political coherence, is the way he is manipulated and diminished by the symbolism of the novel. His argument with Ofeyi, a version of the familiar debate between the liberal and the hardline left, is one of the most intractable in modern politics. In Soyinka's novel however the conflict is resolved—but not, unfortunately, through the process of argument. Instead, by pulling symbolic strings, Soyinka lets Ofeyi off the hook and unites him with the Dentist in an abstract fantasy of ideological harmony. The key to this process is Aiyéró with its curiously imprecise ideological significance. At first the reader might be excused for taking Aiyéró and the Dentist to be allegories of two opposed ideological positions familiar in the real world. Had William Morris been an African he would surely have felt at home in the Aiyéró of the beginning of the novel—a 'quaint anomaly', with its village crafts, its community spirit and closeness to the rhythms of nature. Aiyéró, one might assume, represents utopian socialism, and Ahime's and Ofeyi's plan seems to follow this tradition in seeking a gradual and peacefully accomplished 'change of heart' among the people as a whole. The Dentist, on the other hand, seems to be a ruthless philosopher-anarchist out of Dostoevsky or Zola, a romantic apostle of permanent revolution and advocate of violence. It is on this polarisation of ideology that the structure of much of the novel is based. Ofeyi feels himself to be defending his soft, emotional, poetic response to Aiyéró against the grim commitment of the Dentist who scorns his art as 'will-sapping',[65] and advocates only the immediate destruction of the holders of power. There are, it must be conceded, hints of hidden complications. The actual life of the people in Aiyéró is left suggestively hazy. Ahime refers to the violence which has on occasions characterised his people's history. And once the pogroms have started Aiyéró and the Dentist are clearly broadly on the same side. But it still comes as a shock to the reader when it is revealed that the Dentist has all along been an agent of Aiyéró. It *seems* to be a profoundly meaningful shock. But is it? 'Your meeting abroad was no accident'[66] Ahime tells Ofeyi. All along Aiyéró has been educating Ofeyi through the Dentist. The idealism of utopia and the violence of dedicated ideology have actually, it appears, been working in concert. Symbolically this is meaningful. Soyinka is attempting–to adapt his own words about Armah's *Two Thousand Seasons*–a visionary reconstruction of the *present* for the purposes of social direction. He wishes to show all the forces of 'regeneration': utopianism, ruthless revolution and the liberal individual (such as himself) united together in preparation for the coming struggle. And this is what happens at the end of the novel when Ofeyi sets off in company with Ahime and the Dentist.

The problem is that the real discrepancies between these ideological positions are so great that Soyinka can only achieve the desired harmonisation by an ascent into symbolism of such abstraction that it borders on sheer fantasy. After becoming involved in the intense political and moral debate between Ofeyi and the Dentist, which despite its shortcomings *is* real enough, the reader is bound to feel cheated when asked to believe that the ruthless, hard-headed assassin of the novel had, after all, been despatched by a utopian village community to the waiting-room of a foreign airport, simply in order to chat to a liberal dissident, as if by accident. It may be coherent symbolically, but it makes no sense either in realistic terms, or within the ideological debate of the novel as it has developed so far. Indeed in ideological terms its effect is simply to cancel out the Dentist's previous arguments against Ofeyi's liberalism, cogent and forceful though they sometimes were. They are not defeated on their own terms; they are simply ditched when the Dentist identifies himself with Aiyéró. After this revelation symbolism takes over and no further clarification of political ideology is attempted in the novel. If it were the contradictions inherent in this alliance would become apparent. Instead the Dentist abjectly cooperates with Ofeyi's sensitive individualism. Ofeyi is not, after all, the Dentist tells us, a liberal ditherer. He is one of the creative race which will come after the Dentist's selective 'extractions' and reconstruct the nation: ' "Beyond the elimination of men I know to be destructively evil I envisage nothing. What happens after is up to people like you." '[67] The Dentist and his criticisms are thus robbed of their cutting edge. And Ofeyi can indulge his desire to savour the ultimate aesthetico-mystical experience of the massacres, without fear of criticism.

> Ofeyi returned his penetrating look, frankly. 'Each person does what he is best at, remember?'
> The Dentist, recollecting, said 'Touché.'
> 'But it is a little more than that' Ofeyi added. 'I'm sure every man feels the need to seize for himself the enormity of what is happening, of the time in which it is happening. Perhaps deep down I realise that the search [for Iriyise] would immerse me in the meaning of the event, lead me to a new understanding of history.'[68]

Despite his breathtaking assurance about what 'every man' feels, Ofeyi's response to murder and rapine can scarcely be a common one. He 'seizes' their 'enormity', he 'immerses' himself in 'the meaning of the event' (not, one notes, in the event itself), he 'understands history'. The whole thing is cocooned in sensitive discriminations. Ofeyi remarked earlier, in a similar vein: 'I . . . do not believe in violence. But I see it, I recognize it. I must confront it.'[69] 'Immerse', 'understand', 'see', 'recognize', 'confront'—surely any real-life Dentist, not under the control of Soyinka's symbolic pattern, would pounce upon these limp, consumerist, spectator verbs, and ask Ofeyi what they are supposed to mean, uttered in an environment of real murder and anarchy.

A similar simplification for the convenience of the author's self-projection, Ofeyi, can be seen in the portrayal of the women of the novel. Here Soyinka is following (in his own inventive way) the familiar precedent of centuries of masculine condescension and adulation. The female characters in his work are frequently fascinating, but they seldom approach the autonomy of real human beings. They remain the symbols and fantasies of a complex male mind. In the politics of sex Soyinka is a reactionary. Iriyise for example, symbolically rich though she is, is nevertheless conceived entirely in terms of the well-worn stereotypes projected by male desires and fears. She is a strangely disparate compilation of film-star (and procuress), earth-mother and political revolutionary. The basic idea is perhaps thought-provoking. Unfortunately however these elements remain distinct, forced together without sufficient attempt to make them humanly, or even symbolically coherent. The style used to describe her fluctuates between inflated idealisation and knockabout farce. At first she is portrayed in novelettish terms reminiscent of Ekwensi as 'the gin-and-tonic siren from the godless lights of the capital',[70] as with nice comic effect she wins the infatuated attention of the aged Ahime. However the shadowy and undescribed women of Aiyéró immediately take her to their hearts, apparently without intended irony, feeling her to be closely attuned to natural rhythms.

> Her fingers spliced wounded saplings with the ease of a natural healer. Her presence, the women boasted, inspired the rains.[71]

The combination of earth-mother (even a symbol of Nigeria itself) and sophisticated city-dweller is pursued with reckless boldness in the scene where Zaccheus comes to collect her for her tour. Ofeyi watches her shower:

> On Iriyise's head the shower protection, white crimped rubber became a bowl of husked milky grains, a tumulus of icing.[72]

Absurdity is courted with wilful assurance. And the image 'a tumulus of icing' is certainly a credit to Soyinka's originality if to nothing else. Being an advertising man, Ofeyi naturally begins to speculate on the myths which surround relations

157

between the sexes, defending them as fruitful and creative.

> Iriyise, still, except for her eyes which followed Ofeyi's motions, and Ofeyi in the loose white wrap, sanctified by love-stains, prowling her on cat's feet, priest and vestal in mutual adoration. And why not, thought Ofeyi? Vision is eternally of man's own creating. The woman's acceptance, her collaboration in man's vision of life results time and time again in just such periodic embodiments of earth and ideal.

Notice that 'man' creates; woman merely submits to his creativity. Or by studying his needs she contrives to present him with an ideal, 'a harrowing vision of the unattainable'. At the end of this scene Zaccheus neatly encapsulates Iriyise's significance to the male imagination when he exclaims 'Madamadonna'. She is every man's whore and every man's mother. Under the burden of such romantic stereotyping it is not surprising that Iriyise fails to come fully to life as a human being, or even for that matter as a coherent symbol. The most convincing aspect of her portrayal is perhaps the very self-consciousness with which she acts out the role dictated to her by men. On occasions indeed she presents a masterly and realistic study of a certain kind of female psychology. In her role as 'bitch' for example, raging with desire to attract men and full of spite for her rivals.

> Iriyise entered, bitched to the eyes and bitchy as hell. Yes, she muttered, turn all and stare! Men, dribble. Women, turn to stone; I hate your guts and you envy mine. Shrink back into your padded bras and putty brains, it's me—Celestial! . . .
> She heard Ofeyi's voice at her ear. 'What do we have tonight? Duality of the Iridescent Smile—glass splinters for the ladies, love barbs for the men?' [73]

This passage could have been composed by a feminist as a horrifying illustration of the stunted and unfulfilled emotional life to which the unliberated woman condemns herself. This does not however seem to be the lesson that Soyinka intends. Sometimes indeed Ofeyi, Soyinka and the male reader seem to be intended to enjoy the pornographic display which Iriyise mounts for their benefit: for instance when she chases

Aristo about the courtyard in her dressing gown, wielding a coat-hanger, to the amused awe of the men standing around. It is extremely difficult to believe that this creation (and self-creation) of the male-chauvinist imagination is to be taken seriously as a political agent. Iriyise's enmity towards the Cartel in fact seems to be simply a matter of following the lead of her man, who happens to be Ofeyi. She possesses no identity of her own apart from her impact on men. The cartoon quality of her role as the 'cocoa queen' in Ofeyi's advertising campaign seems to dominate her portrayal throughout the novel. She is 'Iridescent', 'Celestial', the kind of exciting sexual creature who signals to her man by means of the number of clips holding her brassiere on the line outside her flat.[74]

Taiila, symbolic representative of the male conception of the opposite of Iriyise—purity, spirituality and renunciation, is even more of a cartoon creation. 'The mystery virgin of a transit lounge'[75] she calls herself on one occasion. This is of course intended as a joke, but it does in fact indicate the level on which Soyinka has conceived her character. She has none of the realistic touches and the hints of irony which to some extent redeem Iriyise's portrayal. Indeed she is never actually portrayed at all. There are a few tantalising (and at first incomprehensible) reminiscences of her meeting with Ofeyi at the airport, and then when she finally emerges into the novel in person in Chapter XII and it seems that we are to learn more about her, the gripping adventure-story of 'Semi-dozen' intervenes, and she is forgotten. Later Soyinka takes her as 'read' and she becomes simply a symbol of purity and compassion. The sexism of her treatment is easily seen in the episode where Ofeyi and she 'confront' suffering in the church refuge in Chapter XIII. Taiila stands out, pure and exquisite, against the background of poeticised suffering, which sets off her spiritual beauty to such advantage.

> Knowledge of death filtered through the crypt, a chilly current through air that had only begun to warm up. The shadowy inmates underwent changes of infinite subtleties, drawing together even more, purging individual fears in the font of shared loss. . . . death spread its cold tentacles through the festering gloom but it bred no fear in

159

the breasts of any. They had seen too much.

... Ofeyi wondered how they looked to all these fugitives, Taiila especially, foreign and beautiful in the midst of such squalor and destitution. Yet her eyes as she rose from that hard death-bed had held such oceans of sadness, reflecting a suffering that he had not thought possible in one so young. A nun's cowl-framed compassion, held and eternalised in a pieta of luminous stone.[76]

The whole experience is sentimentalised by means of spurious rhetoric: 'shadowy inmates', 'death spread its cold tentacles', 'They had seen too much'. Taiila's eyes hold 'oceans of sadness'. Does Ofeyi really want to know how Taiila looked to the fugitives, one wonders. Or does the author merely wish to emphasise the reassuring gulf between the world of the privileged protagonists and that of the refugees? It may not be entirely unfair to compare the motive behind this passage with that behind those advertisements in up-market fashion magazines which show elegant Western or Westernised women lounging in poverty-stricken third world villages, gawped at by picturesque peasants or urchins.

It is in the style of the novel that the key to its various evasions is best sought. The effect of its extraordinary virtuoso mixture of different styles and registers is to put the whole action on to a kind of floating level, like that of an uneasy, half-waking nightmare. Reality is there, often in painful forms, but it is subject to all sorts of unpredictable distortions and dislocations from the troubled imagination of the author. Most uneasy of all perhaps is the peculiar inflated verbiage used in the first chapters to describe the ritual of 'the bright red sluices' in Aiyéró and then the parody of this in the unveiling of the cocoa fountain at Batoki's party. The description of Ahime's slaughter of the fourteen white bulls must surely rank as the weirdest piece of English prose yet to have been produced in Africa. It reminds one of D.H. Lawrence at his loosest and most 'blood-conscious', and is so sophisticatedly and decadently voluptuous, even pornographic, in effect, that doubts arise as to how seriously it is meant to be taken as a description of a healthy village festival.

160

They saw him feel softly within the folds of his cloth, watch [*sic*] his hand emerge with a slender knife, a mere flutist blade, so insubstantial did it appear against the pillared throats of the bulls.

Iriyise beside him, a distant stillness. Her ivory neck-piece had merged with hidden rapids in the bull's [*sic*] convulsive throats. Caryatid and timeless, only the warmth of her fingers reassured him of her living flesh, a willing presence at the altar . . .

[It is contrived to sound almost as though Iriyise herself were about to become a 'willing' *human* sacrifice!]

His knife-hand moved once, slashed deep and drew across the throat. The taut skin parted easily, opening to a layer of translucent membrane, yielding in turn to tendons and a commencement of red mists. Suddenly the white afternoon was showered in a crimson fountain, rising higher and higher, pumping ever upwards to a sun-scorched sky. Ahime stepped back quickly but not so far that the falling spray should not find him. His white vestments bloomed suddenly with small red petals and a long sigh rose, fell and filled the air with whispers of wind and the opening of buds. He moved swiftly now, the sighs of release were woven among the spreading mists, a thousand eyes followed the motions of the priest whose flutist blade was laid again and again to ivory pipes, tuned to invocations of renewal. Opening the vents of a rich elixir, he of the masseur's fingers stooped at each succeeding sluice-gate, a fountain-head covered in rime, his arms were supple streams in a knowing course through ridges bathed in a sun's downwash. He nudged the ridges' streams awake and they joined their tributaries to his fountain-head . . .[77]

There is a strained luridness about this which seems to indicate that the author's imagination is not really happy with what he is saying. Is his extravagant, baroque rhetoric an attempt to convince *himself* of the regenerative power of this blood-sacrifice? The riot of jumbled metaphor and wilful mixing of registers may lead the reader to suspect conscious (or unconscious?) self-parody on the author's part.

. . . a last spriglet of blood blossomed briefly, then the flood was dammed. A last gargle came through a blocked-up drain, a final shudder of love gave all to a passive earth.[78]

Such hints of self-parody abound in the novel and often impart a strained half-hearted weariness to Soyinka's virtuosity. Sometimes, it must be conceded, the element of the grotesque which is introduced by this indecorous style is put to good use.

> A child corpse flew right over the steel arch and plummeted down like a plump wild duck.

> It began with the slaughter of innocents by the Cartel's para-military troops . . . spattering schoolroom walls with brains hot from learning.[79]

The second example here is brilliantly horrific. The mention that the brains are hot is in itself an unexpected and quite realistic detail, and the odd humour of 'from learning' lends a grimly grotesque farce. But much more often the author seems to be aimlessly playing around with his words: making clever phrases with an eloquence which is distinctly offhand.

> Often before the night was over, she barely managed to animate a face of crinkled negligee abandoned on a winter line, frozen in fragile folds.

> . . . pursued then ignored by an eloquence of eyes.

> 'Leave me to track my own spoors on the laterals, Taiila.'[80]

Such strained rhetoric gives the impression of an unhappy failure of conviction in the novel, an impression reinforced by its frequent instances of sheer carelessness: its incorrect use of words and grammatical slips. 'Forbearers' is used twice where the correct word is 'forbears'.[81] 'Lay' is twice used transitively instead of 'laid'.[82] Awkward neologisms occur with no particular reason:

> A face risen from the grey sea approached them. Stratiated by beams it worked pain-strictured lips to bring out words.[83]

There are frequent loose syntactical constructions.

> Rising to his feet a locomotive ran briefly round the rails which someone had placed in his skull . . .

> Glancing back at the poster again he thought how Iriyise was like the food he ate and, in some measure, grown.[84]

At one point Soyinka even writes 'Egbo' for 'Ofeyi'[85] slipping back into an earlier self-projection in a different novel. A certain *impasto* breathlessness and haste have always been a feature of Soyinka's work. The 'wild and Wole idiom'[86]which Bernth Lindfors observed in his juvenilia, persists in later work. But in this novel it is particularly hectic and anxious in its impact.

Behind the nightmarish uneasiness and half-focused rhetoric of the novel lies a radical nervousness, even fear of its subject on the part of the author. At Shage Dam Ofeyi finds his attention running off after irrelevant details in an attempt to take his mind off the implications of the grim reality before him.

> The crane with its low hook seemed poised to fish out the recumbent figures. Ofeyi followed the line of cord to the derrick limb, to its pivot on the roof of a control cabin, down down to its mud-poulticed caterpillar wheels. Concrete mixer cauldrons with their dirt-caked smoke stack . . . he stopped. It was becoming a habit, running lines in his head to stop the negative flow of implications from stark reality.[87]

In a sense the whole novel can be seen as embodying the same process on a larger scale. And this is the key to its strange nightmare coherence in incoherence. The author is (in a wider sense) 'running lines in his head' in order to cut off the negative flow of implications from his theme. It is this element of therapy in the book which must account for the strangely unified and compulsive effect of its farrago of styles, and for its free mixture of symbol, myth, fantasy, realism and caricature.

It is as just such an attempt to distract himself from unpalatable realities that the novel's most persistent symbolic theme—of sacrifice leading to rebirth—is best understood. Ofeyi several times tries to convince himself that the massacres are part of a rhythmic cycle of natural change: the shedding of blood ensuring a subsequent regeneration of society. Sacrifice and self-sacrifice have always been important to Soyinka. The archetypal creative act of Ogun was a self-sacrificial plunge into the unknown. However, the sacrifice motif in Soyinka's work is from the start hedged about with potential ironies and doubts. In *The Strong Breed* Eman is destroyed as a scape-

163

goat, carrying the sins of the old year upon him. But Soyinka seems to hold out no real hope that the village will experience any purification or regeneration as a result of this sacrifice. Ambiguous or deceptive representatives of rebirth abound in Soyinka's work, the child in *A Dance of the Forests* being one of the earliest. Quite frequently they are charlatans, as is the case with the Kadiye in *The Swamp Dwellers* (first performed 1959), Jero in *The Trials of Brother Jero* (1964) and the Professor in *The Road* (1965) with his *agemo* or half-dead familiar, Murano. *Season of Anomy* seems to show Soyinka on the point of rejecting this myth of rebirth as simply a consoling fiction. The blood-sacrifice so uneasily described at the outset of the novel is followed later by a series of ironic parodies, this time with human beings as victims, rather than bulls. The murder and mutilation of the fugitive who throws himself at Ofeyi's car takes on a grotesque ritual quality, as does the burning of the church at Kuntua (clearly Kaduna). There is an unearthly religious stillness about the scene at Shage. In all these later sacrifices Ofeyi seeks the promise of regeneration. But he does not find it. He is, in the words of *The Man Died*, attempting to 'justify' suffering 'in the form of necessity, wisdom or purification',[88] as tragedy does. He seems to conclude however that this is indeed an 'insidious trap', a consoling patterning of experience which does not correspond with reality. At Shage for instance Ofeyi 'runs' the 'line' of regeneration through his head, but is unable to find relief in it.

> ... perhaps it all seemed part of the churned up earth, part of the clay and humus matrix from which steel hands would later mould new living forms.
> I am lying to myself again he said, seeking barren consolatior..[89]

The parallels implied in Ofeyi's and Iriyise's names with the Greek myth of Orpheus and Euridyce also suggest that any rebirth is illusory. Euridyce is lost to Hades in the legend, and at the end of the novel Iriyise is in a coma. Howevere there *is* faint hope in Soyinka's version. And for all his doubts about the sacrificial pattern of death and rebirth Soyinka does cling to it throughout. The very last words of the novel imply new hope through suffering. 'In the forests life began to stir.' But here again one encounters Soyinka's complexity of style. Surely such a banal cliché ending must be ironic? As with so much else in the novel the reader is left with the dissatisfied question: how seriously are we meant to take it?

## 'Kongi's Harvest' (1965) and 'Ogun Abibimañ' (1976)

Soyinka's political interests are, as we have seen, by no means confined to his native land. And in two of his imaginative works, widely separated in his career, he has turned to political themes from outside Nigeria: the play *Kongi's Harvest*, and the poem *Ogun Abibimañ*. Both concern resistance to political tyranny; but their different contexts and different literary forms produce widely different artistic results. The theme of *Kongi's Harvest*—the tyranny of some black African rulers—allows Soyinka none of the clear and vehement rhetoric that we find in the later poem, whose theme is the tyranny of white over black. In the context of white racism and the liberation of 'the Black Peoples' Soyinka need feel no qualm about advocating revolutionary violence, even while he recognises the suffering that will be caused by it. But when the oppression is not 'from outside', but *by* blacks as well as *of* blacks, his judgement cannot be so decisive. More simply, the actual physical struggle against white rule in Africa is now confined to the distant South, while Soyinka is only too aware of the complex particularities of various Kongisms far closer to home, in East and West Africa.

The strongest aspect of *Kongi's Harvest* is its vigorous, topical satire on Kongism; it is weak and confused when it comes to suggestions for positive action. By the time the play was written the concept of the 'father of the nation' fostered by many African rulers upon independence, was in danger of degenerating in many cases into a 'cult of personality'. Kongi is a generalised and symbolic figure, and Soyinka does not mean to satirise any one particular ruler. Nevertheless several aspects of Kongi do call to mind Kwame Nkrumah of Ghana, who at this time was increasingly resorting to emotive rhetoric and political repression in an attempt to hold off the collapse of his regime (it fell in February, 1966). Nkrumah's speeches frequently show a megalomania comparable to that of Kongi:

> The Convention People's Party [which he founded and led] is Ghana, and Ghana is the Convention People's Party. [90]

The play was first performed in April, 1965, in Dakar, the capital of Senegal, a nation which like Kongi's Ismaland proclaims an official state philosophy which is largely the creation of its President. It would be wrong to press such parallels too far however. The play's political satire works on the level of ideas and principles rather than specific applications.

The form of *Kongi's Harvest*, with its caricatures, its pointed satirical songs and loose structure, recalls Brecht. Indeed it would perhaps be truer to its spirit in some respects to call it a 'revue' or 'cabaret' rather than a 'play'. Brash humour and broad caricature are its most effective satirical vehicles: in the raucously sarcastic opening songs for example:

> I cannot counter words, oh
> I cannot counter words of
> A rediffusion set
> My ears are sore
> But my mouth is *agbayun*
> For I do not bandy words
> No I do not bandy words
> With a government loudspeaker. [91]

There is little attempt to capture the 'illusion of reality'. The characters are flat, illustrating in set 'sketches' the political message. The 'Reformed Aweri' for instance, Kongi's updated version of the council of elders, are public relations men, cooking up an acceptable 'image' for Kongism:

> The emphasis of our generation is—youth. Our image therefore should be a kind of youthful elders of the state. A conclave of modern patriarchs. [92]

Like Nkrumah, Kongi writes many of his books by proxy, a

source of dissension among the Aweri, each of whom is eager to write the next. So Kongi is compelled to take the Secretary's advice to 'write more books. Write enough to go round all of them.'[93] In such broad, farcical satire, full of 'gags', the actors may 'play up to' the audience, free from the decorums of more closely structured drama. There is great vigour in this dramatic mode. But there is also a certain tendency for satirical seriousness to be swamped by the continuous liveliness of the theatrical action. As the play develops, Kongi's megalomania takes on a kind of endearing absurdity, similar to that of Chaplin's Great Dictator, and like Chaplin's creation, he too becomes at times a figure of pure fun rather than of political satire. This results partly from the fact that we do not see much of the concrete effect of Kongi's policy on his society. His philosophy is seen less in terms of its social impact than of the moral deterioration which it brings about within Kongi himself. There is for example his absurd, even pathetic, passion for having public buildings and dams named after him, and the childish (or lunatic) petulance of his claim that he himself is the Spirit of Harvest in whose honour the Festival of the New Yam is held:

KONGI        [*violently.*] : I *am* the Spirit of Harvest. [*The Aweri stir.*]
SECRETARY:   S-sh. They are waking up.
KONGI        [*alarmed, looks round wildly.*] : Who? The people? [*Recovers slowly, angrily begins to climb the steps leading to his cell.*][94]

So far the bearing of the play is clear enough. It is when Soyinka comes to treat political opposition to such Kongism that the lack of such certainties as we find in *Ogun Abibimañ* becomes obvious. The problem centres on the characters of Daodu, a farmer and nephew of the deposed Oba, and Segi, daughter of an opposition leader, night-club hostess and earth-mother—an earlier version of Iriyise. Soyinka seems strangely reluctant to reveal (or perhaps to decide himself) what political action these revolutionaries are planning for the New Yam Festival. At times it seems that they intend to

167

assassinate Kongi. When the Secretary insists that Segi cannot set up a women's organisation without Kongi's permission she replies with heavy meaning: 'We can seek approval—later —if it is still necessary.'[95] Then, during the Festival, Daodu remarks grimly that in a few more moments the sleeping Kongi 'will be woken up. And then it will be too late.'[96] Such remarks seem to imply an assassination, or at least a revolt of some kind. Eldred Jones takes the view that Segi's father, newly escaped from prison, is the intended assassin, and that is why the plan comes to nothing when he is killed.[97] But if this is the plan why do neither Daodu nor Segi mention it? And why are indications given that their intentions are non-violent? At one point Segi even exhorts Daodu not to preach violence in his speech at the Festival: 'It will be enough that you erect a pulpit against him, even for one moment.'[98] These are scarcely the words of a woman intent on assassination. Up to the very last Daodu and Segi seem racked by liberal self-doubts, uncertain, even afraid of action. 'After all, only a little speech. Nothing need come of it.'[99] All this suggests strongly that they are planning a moral rather than a physical confrontation of Kongi. What is the explanation of these strange contradictions? Could it be that Soyinka, with his usual reluctance to countenance the use of violence, even for revolutionary ends, is himself hovering (as he hovers a decade later in *Season of Anomy*), undecided whether to commit his characters to it or not?

The resolution of the play does in the event avoid any violence on the part of the revolutionaries. The confrontation is a moral one, as Segi presents Kongi with the harvest of his rule—her father's head—in place of the new yam. Theatrically effective though this is, the political impact which it makes in the play is implausible. A little surprisingly, in view of what we know of him, Kongi is struck with 'speechless terror' when he sees the head.[100] This may perhaps be explicable in terms of a moral awakening on the tyrant's part. He was after all—Segi has told us—a 'great man' in the past, and also Segi's lover. So presumably he does possess humane sensibilities. He may also be experiencing religious dread at this crucial symbolic desecration of the ritual. It is this religious aspect which must be invoked to explain the reaction of the people at large, in whose eyes, as we gather from the drolly cheerful epilogue, Kongi is now discredited. There is however a lack of definition about Kongi's downfall. Without the Secretary's confirmation that after the Festival Kongi is 'a ruined man'[101] the audience could easily fail to gather that his power has been destroyed. The play's political resolution has been accomplished so much on theatrical rather than thematic terms that it is unclear exactly what it has resolved. Soyinka has shelved the embarrassing problem of revolutionary violence by dramatic trickery. First Segi's father's head is produced as a brilliantly theatrical *deus ex machina*. Then, under cover of this shock-tactic, Soyinka is able to pass off Segi's melodramatically forceful gesture as some kind of meaningful political defeat of the tyrant. It would be comforting to be able to accept the play's apparent lesson: that the Kongis of this world can be defeated by means of carefully staged public demonstrations of their wickedness. It is to be feared however that such non-violent moral victories over oppression will remain somewhat easier to accomplish on the stage than in the real world. The sterner answers of *Ogun Abibimañ* would seem to carry more conviction.

*Ogun Abibimañ* is perhaps Soyinka's most impressive essay in poetry, showing less of the undisciplined riot of mixed metaphor which mars both *Idanre* (1967) and *A Shuttle in the Crypt* (1972). The poem's subject—the approaching liberation of the blacks of south Africa, symbolising the final liberation of 'the Black Nation'[102]—must in large measure account for this greater control and discipline. It is a theme of such breadth and simplicity as to preclude confusion or oversubtlety. To a black African the moral and political issue is too clear and too urgent for equivocation. Soyinka indeed has even expressed a certain envy of the South African writer, whose problems are so much clearer than those of the politically free African:

For the South African still has the right to hope; and this prospect

169

of a future yet uncompromised by failure on his own part, in his own right, is something which has lately ceased to exist for other African writers.[103]

To some extent Soyinka's very choice of subject in this poem restores 'the right to hope' which is so absent from most of his work. And it lacks his usual tortured sense of 'compromise' and 'failure'. The poem, inspired by Mozambique's war against the white Rhodesian regime, takes the form of a direct call to action. Ogun Abibimañ (in Akan: 'Ogun of the Black Peoples') is about to awake, and like the Zulu leader Shaka, raise 'the city of man in commonweal'.[104] And, as was the case with Shaka, the process will inevitably involve violence. The poem contains passages of forthright lucidity rare in Soyinka's work.

> Sanctions followed Dialogue, games
> Of time-pleading.
> And Sharpeville followed Dialogue
> And Dialogue
> Chased its tail, a dogged dog
> Dodging the febrile barks
> Of Protest—
> Always from beyond the fence.
> Sharpeville
> Bared its teeth, and *that*
> Proved no sleeping dog
> Though the kind world let it lie. [105]

In thise case Soyinka's liking for word-play is effective, lending vigour and bite. And the passages of denser metaphor and allusion never become clogged, expressing complex emotion with passionate dignity.

> When, safely distanced, throned in saintly
> Censure, the prophet's voice possesses you—
> *Mere anarchy is loosed upon the world* et cetera
> Remember too, the awesome beauty at the door of birth.
> Labour is holy—behold our midwives with
> The dark wine and black wafers of communion,
> Ministering to history, delivering the missing
> Chapter of the text. [106]

170

# 6 Prospects

There now exists a fairly considerable body of literature written by Nigerians in English and published mainly in England. This literature is studied in 'Commonwealth Literature' and 'African Studies' courses throughout the English-speaking world. Its significance in the context of Nigeria itself is however still a matter of some uncertainty: as is its possible future development. As we have seen, English is by historical accident the only language which at present unites the various peoples of Nigeria; the indigenous languages having largely until now divided them. The English language is thus a pragmatic necessity for Nigerian unity. In some ways this is an unfortunate situation. English in pre-independence and immediately post-independence Nigeria has tended to be the property of a small elite, educated very much along British lines and to a significant extent in Britain.[1] The more important writers in English, for example, share very similar educational backgrounds. Soyinka, Achebe, John Pepper Clark, Amadi, Okigbo and the younger novelist Kole Omotoso all studied in Nigeria's oldest institution for higher education at Ibadan, in the 1950s and 1960s. Founded in 1948 as the University College, Ibadan, 'an extension in Nigeria of the University of London',[2] its original function was to educate the new black elite which would eventually take over from the colonialist. It became an autonomous University in 1962. Several writers have studied in Britain itself, Soyinka (like Ngugi) at Leeds University, Aluko and Ekwensi in London, and Flora Nwapa and Kole Omotoso in Edinburgh. Only Tutuola and Okara, among prominent writers, have no such background in higher education. The first generation of

171

Nigerian writers is thus the unique product of the particular conditions of a period of decolonisation. And one might ask whether future generations will retain this close association with the educational and cultural perspectives of the ex-colonial power. If not, what alternative perspectives will be developed in years to come, what kind of English will be spoken and written in Nigeria, and what will be the importance of English in Nigerian society and culture?

The future shape of Nigerian literature will depend on two factors: the relative status of English and the indigenous languages (actual rather than official), and—of prime importance—the nature and quality of Nigerian education. We may be inclined to dismiss, with J.P. Clark, the claim that the English language and literature in English will (or should) die out in Nigeria as the indigenous languages reassert themselves.[3] But such a wish is bound to come naturally to many self-respecting Nigerians, conscious of the continuing eclipse of their own culture by that of the English-speaking world—Britain, and now increasingly, the United States. The government's policy that all children should learn one other indigenous language apart from their own, might eventually create the conditions for literatures in Hausa, Ibo or Yoruba with a wide and popular *Nigerian* audience—truly Nigerian literatures in native Nigerian languages. This can only be a long-term possibility however, and it must seem inevitable that English and literature in English will retain their centrality for the foreseeable future. To the thinking Nigerian a more immediate and urgent question might seem to be the *quality* of the English used in Nigeria. If good spoken and written English could be inculcated more widely at all levels of society, rather than being confined to a limited elite as hitherto, then the language might begin to express Nigerian society and culture in far more various and original ways than it does at present. The term 'Nigerian English' might cease to imply 'bad English' and come to indicate a genuine new form of the language with its own idioms and nuances. However, as with the desired spread of indigenous languages, everything depends on efficient and widespread education. And at present it is generally recognised that standards of English and of English teaching in Nigeria are extremely variable. In his inaugural lecture at Ife University delivered on January 25, 1979, Professor Afolayan cited an essay by a Grade Two teacher which contained not a single grammatical sentence. Moreover, any widespread improvement in education is hampered by the soaring birth-rate. Whatever extensions and improvements in education may be made are likely to be swamped by the massive and inexorable growth of the school population. It is here perhaps, more than anywhere else, in the education of Nigeria's diverse and increasing population, that the key to its political and cultural future must lie.

With the installation of a new civilian government in October, 1979, after thirteen years of military rule, a new phase in Nigeria's political, and perhaps cultural, history has begun. There is now new scope for political debate and discussion, which were inevitably inhibited under military rule, however benign it may have been. There have been encouraging signs. The dispute in the Constituent Assembly early in 1978 over whether the new constitution should provide for a Federal Sharia Court of Appeal for Islamic law, separate from the secular court, seemed to threaten a serious regional clash between North and South.[4] But in the event the issue did not cause any lasting disruption. Moreover laws now exist to prevent the regional bias of political parties which so marred the First Republic. And it is generally agreed that the 1979 elections took place with unprecedented discipline and fairness. It remains to be seen however how successfully the new administration under Shehu Shagari will cope with the nation's problems. It also remains to be seen what tone the newly revived political life of Nigeria will now take, and what response it will find from future writers who treat political themes. The politicians and writers of the immediate post-colonial period are now giving way to the members of a new generation, who do not remember their country as it was before independence, and who may, perhaps, find more success in the search for a genuine Nigerian political and cultural identity.

173

# Chapter Notes

## 1 Perspectives

1. *For Lancelot Andrewes: Essays on Style and Order* (London: Faber and Gwyer, 1928), p. ix.

2. *What Is Literature?*, translated by Bernard Frechtman (London: Methuen, 1967), p. 214.

3. Translated as *The African Child* by James Kirkup (London: Fontana, 1959).

4. 'The Role of the Writer in a New Nation', *Nigeria Magazine*, 81 (1964); reprinted in *African Writers on African Writing*, ed. G.D. Killam (London: Heinemann, 1973), p. 9.

5. 'The Novelist as Teacher', *New Statesman*, Jan. 29, 1965; reprinted in Killam, *African Writers*, p. 3.

6. Killam, p. 9.

7. *Two Thousand Seasons* (Nairobi: East African Publishing House, 1973), p. 2.

8. *TTS*, p. 18.

9. *TTS*, pp. 4-5.

10. 'African Socialism: Utopian or Scientific?' *Présence Africaine*, 64, 4th. Quarterly, 1967, p. 15.

11. Wole Soyinka, *Myth, Literature and the African World* (Cambridge: Cambridge University Press, 1976), p. 106.

12. *Cahier d'un Retour au Pays Natal: Return to My Native Land*, translated by Emile Snyder (Paris: Editions Présence Africaine, 1971), p. 120. Gerald Moore (*Seven African Writers*, London: Oxford University Press, corrected edn., 1966) translates the enigmatic *Eia* as 'Hurray', which strikes a note of affirmative heartiness foreign to the poem. John Berger and Anna Bostock (London: Penguin Books, 1969, p. 76) preserve the indefiniteness of the exclamation by leaving it as 'Heia', but mistranslate *la douleur aux pis de larmes* ('grief at the udders of tears') as 'Of tears and the worst pain', which robs Césaire of his surrealism.

13. Soyinka, *MLAW*, p. 127.

14. Quoted in *MLAW*, p. 129.

15. *MLAW*, p. 129.

16. From a speech delivered in Oxford in October 1961; quoted by K.A. Busia, *Africa in Search of Democracy* (London: Routledge and Kegan Paul, 1967), p. 44.

17. From a speech delivered in France in October 1959; quoted by

Busia, p. 43.

18. Killam, pp. 3-4.

19. Busia, p. 46.

20. *Nocturnes*, translated by John Reed and Clive Wake (London: Heinemann, 1969), p. 14.

21. *Nocturnes*, p. 20.

22. *Nocturnes*, p. 12.

23. *MLAW*, p. 130.

24. *MLAW*, pp. 138-9.

25. *MLAW*, p. 135.

26. Armah, 'African Socialism', p. 28.

27. Kwame Nkrumah, *I Speak of Freedom* (London, 1961: Panaf Books, 1973) p. xii.

28. Frantz Fanon, *The Wretched of the Earth*, translated by Constance Farrington (London: McGibbon and Kee, 1965; Penguin Books, 1967), p. 188.

29. See for example Basil Davidson, *Can Africa Survive?* (New York: Atlantic Monthly Press, 1974), pp. 27-9.

30. Fanon, p. 120.

31. Davidson, pp. 34-5.

32. Fanon, p. 125.

33. Quoted in Claude Wauthier, *The Literature and Thought of Modern Africa*, translated by Shirley Kay (London: Pall Mall Press, 1966), p. 250.

34. *Ujamaa: Essays on Socialism* (Dar-es-Salaam: Oxford University Press, 1968), pp. 11-12.

35. Margaret Peil, *Nigerian Politics: The People's View* (London: Cassell, 1976), p. 7.

36. Peil, p. 188.

37. Peil, p. 65.

38. Peil, p. 138.

39. Peil, p. 139.

40. Davidson, p. 52.

41. *Awo: The Autobiography of Chief Obafemi Awolowo* (Cambridge: Cambridge University Press, 1960), p. 206.

42. Margery Perham, quoted in Davidson, p. 60.

43. Ruth First, *The Barrel of a Gun: Political Power in Africa and the Coup D'Etat* (London: Allen Lane The Penguin Press, 1970; Penguin African Library, 1972), p. 144.

44. *The Story of Nigeria* (London: Faber and Faber, 1962; 4th. edn., 1978), p. 23.

45. *Arrow of God* (London: Heinemann, 1964), p. 215.

46. See *Awo*, Chapter 13, pp. 185-212.

47. Taken from a tape of Nzeogwu's broadcast over Radio Kaduna, Jan. 15, 1966; quoted in First, *The Barrel of a Gun*, p. 285.

48. *No Longer At Ease* (London: Heinemann, 1960), p. 103.

49. *Beautiful Feathers* (London, Hutchinson, 1963: Heinemann African Writers Series, 1971), p. 5.

50. Sunday Anozie, *Christopher Okigbo* (Evans Brothers, 1972), pp. 10-11.

51. *The Man Died: Prison Notes of Wole Soyinka* (London: Rex Collings, 1972; Penguin Books, 1975); p. 161.

52. *TMD*, pp. 166-70.

53. *TMD*, p. 182.

54. *TMD*, p. 182.

55. 'Nigeria: The Issue of States', *Africa*, 44, April 1975.

56. See the Government White Paper, 'National Policy on Education' (Lagos: Federal Ministry of Information Printing Division, 1977), p. 15.

57. First, p. 40.

58. Busia, *Africa in Search*, p. 50.

59. *West Africa*, Jan. 29, 1966, p. 114.

60. The phrase means *A Society of the Descendants of Oduduwa*, Oduduwa being the Yoruba god of creation.

61. Ahmadu Bello, *My Life* (Cambridge: Cambridge University Press, 1962), p. 6.

62. *My Life*, p. 82.

63. *My Life*, p. 131.

64. *My Life*, p. 101.

65. *My Life*, p. 191.

66. *My Life*, p. 227.

67. *My Life*, p. 229.

68. *My Life*, p. 16.

69. *My Life*, p. 135-6.

70. *My Life*, p. 150.

71. *My Life*, p. 85.

72. *My Life*, p. 112.

73. *My Life*, p. 206 and pp. 215-6.

74. *My Life*, p. 216. Bello's treatment of the minorities issue may be contrasted with that of Awolowo (*Awo*, Chapters 12 and 13), which aims at objectivity.

75. *My Life*, p. 232.

76. For example, *My Life*, p. 126 and p. 194.

77. *My Life*, p. 159.

78. *My Life*, p. 19.

79. *My Life*, p. 86.

80. *My Life*, p. 125.

81. *My Life*, p. 178.

82. Nnamdi Azikiwe, *My Odyssey* (London: C. Hurst and Company, 1970), p. 94.

83. *Awo*, p. 71.

84. *Awo*, p. 109.

85. *My Odyssey*, p. 11.

86. *Awo*, p. 122.

87. *My Odyssey*, p. 175.

88. *My Odyssey*, p. 45.

89. *Awo*, p. 102.

90. *My Odyssey*, pp. 44-5.

91. *Ashanti Pioneer*, September 6, 1961; quoted by First, p. 182.

92. *Awo*, p. 309.

93. *Awo*, p. 304.

94. *Awo*, p. 255.

95. *Awo*, p. 283.

96. *Awo*, p. 104 and p. 106.

97. A.A. Mazrui, *Political Values and the Educated Class in Africa* (London: Heinemann, 1978), p. 72.

98. *My Life*, p. 126.

99. *Awo*, pp. 35, 152 and 94.

100. *My Odyssey*, p. xi.

101. *My Odyssey*, pp. 77, 250 and 384.

102. *My Odyssey*, p. 105.

## 2 Literature and the politics of language

1. See Michael Crowder, *The Story of Nigeria* (London: Faber and Faber, 1962; 4th. edn., 1978), pp. 13-15. Various more exact estimates have been made, ranging from 200 to 380. Much depends upon the precise distinction made between a 'language' and a 'dialect'.

2. Denis Herbstein, *The Sunday Times* (London), June 20, 1976, reported that the death toll in anti-Afrikaans riots had reached 100, with more than 1,000 wounded:

> ... there are only a handful of teachers in the whole of Soweto (population one and a half million) who can teach mathematics proficiently in Afrikaans. Even in schools where there was no Afrikaans-speaking maths master and instruction was permitted in

177

English, the textbooks issued [in 1975] were in Afrikaans.

3. *Tell Freedom* (London: Faber and Faber, 1954).

4. *The African Image* (London: Faber and Faber, 1962; revised edn., 1974), p. 132.

5. Translated as *Mission to Kala* by Peter Green (London: Heinemann, 1958).

6. 'The Soul of Africa in Guinea', *African Literature and the Universities: Papers presented at the First Festival of Negro Arts, Dakar* (Ibadan: Ibadan University Press, 1965); reprinted in *African Writers on African Writing*, ed. G.D. Killam (London: Heinemann, 1973), p. 164.

7. *Léopold Sédar Senghor: Prose and Poetry*, selected and translated by John Reed and Clive Wake (London: Oxford University Press, 1965), p. 95.

8. 'The Writers Speak', *African Literature and the Universities*, reprinted in Killam, *African Writers*, p. 150.

9. The play on the different languages in this scene, so effective on the screen, cannot be conveyed satisfactorily through the written word, and is omitted from the novel version of *Xala* (translated by Clive Wake, London: Heinemann, 1976).

10. Translated by Karen C. Chapman (London: Heinemann, 1971).

11. 'The Role of the Writer in a New Nation', *Nigeria Magazine*, 81 (1964); reprinted in Killam, *African Writers*, p. 12.

12. 'Aspects of Nigerian Drama', *Nigeria Magazine*, 89 (1966), reprinted in Killam, p. 31.

13. Killam, p. 31.

14. It has been suggested that Ngugi's imprisonment in 1977-8 'for the possession of Chinese and other Communist literature banned in Kenya', was brought upon him by the satire on identifiable politicians contained in his drama in Kikuyu, *Ngahiku Ndenda*, which played to uneducated audiences. This, it is thought, was considered far more dangerous by the authorities than the novel in English, *Petals of Blood*, with its middle class and international audience. See Chris Wanjala, 'The silenced satirist', *The Guardian* (London), March 6, 1978, p. 17.

15. Quoted by Claude Wauthier, *The Literature and Thought of Modern Africa*, translated by Shirley Kay (London: Pall Mall Press, 1966), pp. 44-5.

16. 'National Policy in Education' (Lagos: Federal Ministry of Information Printing Division, 1977), p. 5.

17. Bernth Lindfors (ed.), *Critical Perspectives on Nigerian Literatures* (United States: Three Continents Press, 1975; London: Heinemann, 1979), p. 196.

18. From a letter written to Faber and Faber (London), July 14, 1964; quoted in *A Reader's Guide to African Literature*, ed. Hanz Zell and Helene Silver (London: Heinemann, 1972), p. 196.

19. *The Palm-Wine Drinkard* (London: Faber and Faber, 1952; new edn., 1961), pp. 13-14.

20. *TPWD*, p. 16.

21. 'Language and Sources of Amos Tutuola', *Perspectives on African Literature*, ed. Christopher Heywood (London: Heinemann, 1971), p. 54.

22. Heywood, *Perspectives*, p. 61.

23. *TPWD*, p. 16.

24. *The Observer* (London), July 6, 1952, p. 7; quoted in Zell and Silver, *A Reader's Guide*, p. 196.

25. Detailed description of flora and fauna is in fact totally lacking in Tutuola's work.

26. Margaret Laurence, *Long Drums and Cannons* (London: Macmillan, 1968), p. 147.

27. Charles R. Larson, *The Emergence of African Fiction* (Bloomington, Ind.: Indiana University Press; revised edn., 1972), p. 95.

28. 'Larsony, or Fiction as Criticism of Fiction', *New Classic*, November 1977.

29. 'The writer in a modern African state', *The Writer in Modern Africa*, ed. Per Wastberg (New York, Africana Publishing Corporation, 1969); quoted in Zell and Silver, p. 191.

30. *Why Are We So Blest?* (New York: Doubleday, 1972; London: Heinemann, 1974), p. 119.

31. Quoted in Zell and Silver, p. 191.

32. Heywood, p. 61.

33. Killam, p. 12.

34. Killam, p. 12.

35. *The Sunday Times* (Lagos), July 2, 1978, p. 17.

36. Gabriel Okara, 'African Speech . . . English Words', *Transition*, vol. 3, no.10, 1963; quoted in Zell and Silver, pp. 165-6.

37. *The Voice* (London: Heinemann, 1970), p. 32.

38. *The Voice*, pp. 66-7.

39. *The Voice*, pp. 47-8.

40. 'Where Angels Fear to Tread', *Nigeria Magazine*, 75 (1962); reprinted in Killam, *African Writers*, p. 7.

41. Killam, p. 12.

42. 'The English Language and the African Writer', *Insight*, October/December, 1966, p. 21.

43. *Things Fall Apart* (London: Heinemann, 1966), pp. 3-4.

44. *TFA*, p. 55.

179

45. See Bernth Lindfors, 'The Palm Oil with which Achebe's words are eaten', *African Literature Today*, No. 1, 1968; and Gareth Griffiths, 'Language and Action in the Novels of Chinua Achebe', *African Literature Today*, No. 5, 1971.

46. Bernth Lindfors, 'Achebe on commitment and African writers', *Africa Report*, March 1970, p. 18.

47. '⁷⁻ Language of West African Literature in English', *The English Language in West Africa*, ed. John Spencer, London: Longman, 1971, p. 174.

48. Killam, p. 12.

49. 'The Novelist as Teacher', *New Statesman*, January 29, 1965: reprinted in Killam, p. 4.

50. *Chinua Achebe* (New York: Twayne Publishers Inc., 1970), pp. 15-35.

51. *Heart of Darkness* (London, 1902; Penguin Books, 1973), p. 51.

52. *TFA*, pp. 218-9.

53. From Sartre's Introduction, *Orphée Noir*, to Senghor's *Anthologie de la nouvelle poésie nègre et malgache* (Paris, 1940); quoted in Wauthier, *The Literature and Thought of Modern Africa*, pp. 38-9.

## 3 Democracy and the elite

1. *The Wretched of the Earth*, translated by Constance Farrington (London: McGibbon and Kee, 1965; Penguin Books, 1967), p. 178-9.

2. *Commonwealth Literature* (London: Oxford University Press, 1973), pp. 42-3.

3. *The Novel and Contemporary Experience in Africa* (London: Heinemann, 1977), p. 65.

4. *One Man, One Matchet* (London: Heinemann, 1964), p. 40.

5. *OMOM*, p. 40.

6. *OMOM*, p. 41.

7. *OMOM*, p. 18.

8. *OMOM*, p. 69.

9. *OMOM*, pp. 165-6.

10. *OMOM*, p. 156.

11. *OMOM*, pp. 9-10.

12. *OMOM*, p. 196.

13. *OMOM*, p. 146.

14. *OMOM*, p. 142.

15. *OMOM*, p. 143.

16. *The Novel and Contemporary Experience*, p. 65.

## 4 'Distress and difficulty'

1. *The Wretched of the Earth*, translated by Constance Farrington (London: McGibbon and Kee, 1965; Penguin Books, 1967) , p. 179.

2. *No Longer At Ease* (London: Heinemann, 1960), p. 32.

3. *NLAE*, p. 92.

4. See *West Africa*, March 6, 1978, p. 437.

Many Nigerians were unenthusiastic about the Fair. Some felt that the money spent on the complex—perhaps ₦100m. [about £90m.] —and on recurrent costs could be better spent. What, they asked had Nigeria to sell through this elaborate organization? ... The Head of State ... clearly shared some of these misgivings. To the extent to which the Fair and the site contributed to 'improving our capacity to produce our needs', he said, 'it will be a worthwhile venture.' To the extent that it would provide at Nigeria's cost a showroom for manufacturers from all over the world to make bigger sales which 'do not in any way free us from total dependence on the industrialised economies it would be of doubtful value to us'. For the time being the Head of State agreed, Nigeria would buy far more than she would sell through mounting a trade fair.

5. *NLAE*, p. 98.

6. *NLAE*, p. 97.

7. Fanon, p. 11.

8. *A Man of the People* (London: Heinemann, 1966; reset 1975), p. 37.

9. Eustace Palmer, *An Introduction to the African Novel* (London: Heinemann, 1972), pp. 72-84.

10. Gareth Griffiths, 'Language and Action in the Novels of Chinua Achebe', *African Literature Today*, No. 5, 1971.

11. Palmer, p. 74.

12. Palmer, p. 79.

13. Palmer, p. 73.

14. Palmer, p. 77.

15. *A Man of the People*, p. 9.

16. *AMOTP*, p. 10.

17. Bernth Lindfors, 'The Blind Men and the Elephant', *African Literature Today*, No. 7, 1975, p. 63. Lindfors comments that Griffiths's interpretation of Odili 'is almost the reverse of what the author actually intended in creating his hero'.

18. *AMOTP*, p. 9.

19. *AMOTP*, p. 11.

20. Palmer, p. 79.

21. In a Convocation Lecture given at the University of Ife, December 15, 1978 (not yet published) Achebe drew attention to the fact that from the start of composition it takes at the very least two years for a novel to appear in print. It would be stretching plausibility to imagine a group of soldiers confiding their *coup* plans to a novelist, and then delaying their action for two years or more, so that it might coincide with the appearance of his book.

22. *AMOTP*, p. 148.

23. *NLAE*, p. 21.

24. *AMOTP*, pp. 114-5.

25. *AMOTP*, p. 2.

26. *AMOTP*, p. 2.

27. *AMOTP*, p. 128.

28. J.P. O'Flinn, 'Towards a Sociology of the Nigerian Novel', *African Literature Today*, No. 7, 1975, p. 47.

29. O'Flinn, p. 48.

30. *AMOTP*, pp. 143-4.

31. *AMOTP*, p. 37.

32. *NLAE*, p. 99.

33. *AMOTP*, p. 65.

34. *AMOTP*, p. 123.

35. 'The Voter', *Girls at War and Other Stories* (London: Heinemann, 1972), p. 17.

36. 'The Voter', p. 19.

## 5 The artist and political commitment

1. Gerald Moore, *Wole Soyinka* (London: Evans Brothers Ltd., 1971), p. 79.

2. See Bernth Lindfors, 'The Early Writings of Wole Soyinka', *Critical Perspectives on Nigerian Literatures*, ed. Bernth Lindfors (U.S.: Three Continents Press, 1975; London: Heinemann, 1979), p. 190.

3. Lindfors, 'The Early Writings', p. 165.

4. Quoted in *A Reader's Guide to African Literature*, ed. Hans Zell and Helene Silver (London: Heinemann, 1972), p. 192.

5. *Myth, Literature and the African World* (Cambridge: Cambridge University Press, 1976), pp. ix-x.

6. Eldred Durosimi Jones, *The Writing of Wole Soyinka* (London: Heinemann, 1973), p. 34.

7. Moore, *Wole Soyinka*, p. 85.

8. Ngugi wa Thiong'o, *Homecoming* (London: Heinemann, 1972), p.65.

9. J.P. O'Flinn, 'Towards a Sociology of the Nigerian Novel', *African Literature Today*, No. 7, 1975, p. 48.

10. Moore, p. 75.

11. See 'Professor Soyinka Protests', *Daily Times* (Lagos), April 26, 1978.

12. *The Man Died: Prison Notes of Wole Soyinka* (London: Rex Collings, 1972; Penguin Books, 1975), p. 13.

13. C. Tighe, 'In Detentio Preventione in Aeternum: Soyinka's *A Shuttle in the Crypt*', *Journal of Commonwealth Literature*, Vol. X, No. 3, April 1976, p. 12.

14. Quoted in Zell and Silver, *A Reader's Guide*, p. 192.

15. *The Man Died*, p. 95.

16. *TMD*, p. 20.

17. *TMD*, pp. 179-80.

18. Wole Soyinka, 'And after the Narcissist?', *African Forum*, New York, Vol. 1, No. 4, Spring 1966; quoted in Moore, p. 101.

19. 'The Origins of *A Dance of the Forests*', *African Literature Today*, No. 8, 1976, pp. 66-71.

20. Wole Soyinka, *Five Plays* (London: Oxford University Press, 1964), p. 55.

21. *Five Plays*, pp. 55-6.

22. *Five Plays*, p. 57.

23. *Five Plays*, p. 57.

24. *Five Plays*, p. 82.

25. 'Demoke's Choice in Soyinka's *A Dance of the Forests*', *Journal of Commonwealth Literature*, Vol. X, No. 3, April 1976, pp. 22-7.

26. 'The Fourth Stage', *Myth, Literature and the African World*, p. 145.

27. Translated by John and Necke Mander (London: Merlin Press, 1962).

28. *The Interpreters* (London: André Deutsch, 1965; Heinemann, 1970), p. 178.

29. See *A Portrait of the Artist as a Young Man* (London: 1916; Penguin Books, 1960), pp. 204-5.

30. *The Interpreters*, p. 12.

31. *TI*, p. 11.

32. *TI*, p. 121.

33. *TI*, p. 13.

34. *TI*, p. 14.

35. *TI*, p. 9.

36. *TI*, p. 95.

37. *TI*, p. 98.

38. *TI*, p. 14.
39. S.A. Gakwandi, *The Novel and Contemporary Experience in Africa* (London: Heinemann, 1977), p. 85.
40. *TI*, p. 78.
41. *TI*
42. *TI*, p. 120.
43. *TI*, pp. 130-3.
44. *TI*, p. 127.
45. Gakwandi, *The Novel and Contemporary Experience*, pp. 82-3.
46. *TI*, pp. 222-4.
47. *The Man Died*, p. 88.
48. *TMD*, p. 88.
49. *TMD*, p. 89.
50. *TMD*, p. 88.
51. *TMD*, p. 90.
52. *TMD*, p. 90.
53. Frantz Fanon, *The Wretched of the Earth*, translated by Constance Farrington (London: McGibbon and Kee, 1965; Penguin Books, 1967), p. 179.
54. Fanon, p. 186.
55. *Season of Anomy* (London: Rex Collings, 1973), p. 86.
56. *SA*, p. 137.
57. *SA*, p. 159.
58. *SA*, p. 27.
59. *SA*, p. 170.
60. *SA*, p. 275-6.
61. *SA*, p. 134.
62. *SA*, pp. 190-1.
63. *SA*, p. 141.
64. *SA*, p. 180.
65. *SA*, p. 102.
66. *SA*, p. 216.
67. *SA*, p. 112.
68. *SA*, p. 218.
69. *SA*, p. 100.
70. *SA*, p. 7.
71. *SA*, p. 20.
72. *SA*, p. 82.
73. *SA*, pp. 38 and 41.
74. *SA*, p. 60.
75. *SA*, p. 98.
76. *SA*, pp. 270-1.
77. *SA*, pp. 16-17.

78. *SA*, p. 17.
79. *SA*, pp. 194 and 110.
80. *SA*, pp. 145, 268 and 98.
81. *SA*, pp. 181 and 273.
82. *SA*, pp. 270 and 316.
83. *SA*, p. 269.
84. *SA*, pp. 308 and 58.
85. *SA*, p. 152.
86. Bernth Lindfors, 'The Early Writings of Wole Soyinka', p. 176.
87. *SA*, p. 173.
88. *TMD*, p. 90.
89. *SA*, p. 173.
90. *I Speak of Freedom* (London, 1961; Panaf Books, 1973), p. 209.
91. *Kongi's Harvest* (London: Oxford University Press, 1967), p. 2.
92. *KH*, p. 12.
93. *KH*, p. 35.
94. *KH*, p. 36.
95. *KH*, p. 75.
96. *KH*, p. 79.
97. Jones, *The Writing of Wole Soyinka*, p. 87. '. . . the sound of gunfire heralds the death of Segi's father who, it transpires, was to have done the crucial act. The plot obviously fails . . .'
98. *KH*, p. 46.
99. *KH*, p. 76.
100. *KH*, p. 84.
101. *KH*, p. 87.
102. *Ogun Abibimañ* (London: Rex Collings, 1976), p. 23.
103. Quoted in Ruth First, *The Barrel of a Gun* (London: Allen Lane The Penguin Press, 1970; Penguin African Library, 1972), p. 12.
104. *OA*, p. 15.
105. *OA*, p. 6.
106. *OA*, p. 21.

## 6 Prospects

1. John Pepper Clark studied for a year in the United States, at Princeton.
2. *Commonwealth Universities Yearbook: 1977-8* (London: The Association of Commonwealth Universities, 1977), Vol. 3, p. 1830.
3. See above, p. 72.
4. See 'Walkout Protest over Sharia', *West Africa*, April 17, 1978; and 'Obasanjo warning to Assembly members', *West Africa*, April 24, 1978.

# Select Bibliography

I have included only material immediately relevant to my theme.

## Primary Nigerian sources

Achebe, Chinua: *Things Fall Apart*, London: Heinemann, 1958
    *No Longer At Ease*, London: Heinemann, 1960.
    *Arrow of God*, London: Heinemann, 1964.
    *A Man of the People*, London: Heinemann, 1966.
    *Girls at War and Other Stories*, London: Heinemann, 1972.
Aluko, Timothy M.: *One Man, One Matchet*, London: Heinemann, 1964.
    *Chief the Honourable Minister*, London: Heinemann, 1970.
Amadi, Elechi: *The Concubine*, London: Heinemann, 1966.
    *Sunset in Biafra*, London: Heinemann, 1973.
Awolowo, Obafemi: *Awo*, Cambridge: Cambridge University Press, 1960.
Azikiwe, Nnamdi: *My Odyssey*, London: C. Hurst and Co., 1970.
Bello, Ahmadu: *My Life*, Cambridge: Cambridge University Press, 1962.
Clark, John Pepper: *America, Their America*, London: André Deutsch, 1964.
    *Ozidi*, Oxford: Oxford University Press, 1966.
    *Casualties*, London: Longman, 1970.
Ekwensi, Cyprian: *Beautiful Feathers*, London: Heinemann, 1962.
    *Survive the Peace*, London: Heinemann, 1976.
Ladipo, Duro: *Three Yoruba Plays*, transl. Ulli Beier, Ibadan: Mbari Publications, 1964.
Mezu, S. Okechukwu: *Behind the Rising Sun*, London: Heinemann, 1971.
Munonye, John: *The Only Son*, London: Heinemann; 1966.
    *Obi*, London: Heinemann, 1969.
Nwankwo, Nkem: *Danda*, London: André Deutsch, 1964.
Nwapa, Flora: *Efuru*, London: Heinemann, 1966.
Okara, Gabriel: *The Voice*, London: André Deutsch, 1964.
Okigbo, Christopher: *Labyrinths*, London: Heinemann, 1971.
Omotoso, Kole: *The Edifice*, London: Heinemann, 1970.
Rotimi, Ola: *Kurunmi*, Oxford: Oxford University Press, 1971.
    *The Gods Are Not to Blame*, Oxford: Oxford University Press, 1971.
Soyinka, Wole: *Five Plays*, Oxford: Oxford University Press, 1964.
    *The Road*, Oxford: Oxford University Press, 1965.

*The Interpreters*, London: André Deutsch, 1965.

*Kongi's Harvest*, Oxford: Oxford University Press, 1967.

*Idanre*, London: Methuen, 1967.

*Madmen and Specialists*, London: Methuen, 1971.

*A Shuttle in the Crypt*, London: Rex Collings and Eyre Methuen, 1972.

*The Man Died*, London: Rex Collings, 1972.

*Season of Anomy*, London: Rex Collings, 1973.

*Myth, Literature and the African World*, Cambridge: Cambridge University Press, 1976.

*Ogun Abibiman*, London: Rex Collings, 1976.

Tutuola, Amos: *The Palm-Wine Drinkard*, London: Faber and Faber, 1952.

*My Life in the Bush of Ghosts*, London: Faber and Faber, 1954.

Obiechina, Emmanuel N. (ed.): *Onitsha Market Literature*, London: Heinemann, 1972.

## Secondary sources

Abrahams, Peter: *Tell Freedom*, London: Faber and Faber, 1954.

Achebe, Chinua: *Morning Yet On Creation Day: Essays*, London: Heinemann, 1977.

Akpan, Ntieyong U.: *The Struggle for Secession, 1966-1970*, London: Frank Cass; second edition 1976.

Aluko, Samuel: 'Nigeria: The Issue of States', *Africa* No. 44, April 1975.

Anozie, Sunday O.: *Christopher Okigbo: Creative Rhetoric*, London: Evans Brothers, 1972.

Armah, Ayi Kwei: *Two Thousand Seasons*, Nairobi: East African Publishing House, 1973.

*Why Are We So Blest?*, London: Heinemann, 1974.

'African Socialism: Utopian or Scientific?', *Présence Africaine*, 64, 4th. Quarterly, 1967.

'Larsony, or Fiction as Criticism of Fiction', *New Classic*, Nov. 1977.

Beti, Mongo: *Mission to Kala*, transl. Peter Green, London: Heinemann, 1958.

Busia, Kofi A.: *Africa in Search of Democracy*, London: Routledge and Kegan Paul, 1967.

187

Carroll, David: *Chinua Achebe*, New York: Twayne Publishers Inc., 1970.

Cary, Joyce: *Aissa Saved*, London: Michael Joseph, 1949.

   *Mister Johnson*, London: Penguin Books, 1962.

Césaire, Aimé: *Cahier d'un Retour au Pays Natal: Return to My Native Land*, transl. Emile Snyder, Paris: Editions Présence Africaine, 1971.

Conrad, Joseph: *Heart of Darkness*, London: Penguin Books, 1973.

Crowder, Michael: *The Story of Nigeria*, London: Faber and Faber; 4th. edn., 1978.

Davidson, Basil: *Can Africa Survive?*, New York: Atlantic Monthly Press, 1974.

Fage, J.D.: *A History of West Africa*, Cambridge: Cambridge University Press; 4th. edn., 1969.

Fanon, Frantz: *The Wretched of the Earth*, transl. Constance Farrington, London: Penguin Books, 1967.

First, Ruth: *The Barrel of a Gun: Political Power in Africa and the Coup d'État*, London: Penguin Books, 1972.

Gakwandi, Shatto A.: *The Novel and Contemporary Experience in Africa*, London: Heinemann, 1977.

Gibbs, James: 'The Origins of *A Dance of the Forests*', *African Literature Today*, No. 8, 1976.

Gleason, Judith I.: *This Africa*, Evanston: Northwestern University Press, 1965.

Griffiths, Gareth: 'Language and Action in the Novels of Chinua Achebe', *African Literature Today*, No. 5, 1971.

Heywood, Christopher (ed.): *Perspectives on African Literature*, London: Heinemann, 1971.

Jones, Eldred D.: *The Writing of Wole Soyinka*, London: Heinemann, 1973.

Killam, G.D. (ed.): *African Writers on African Writing*, London: Heinemann, 1973.

   *The Writings of Chinua Achebe*, London: Heinemann; revised edn., 1977.

Larson, Charles R.: *The Emergence of African Fiction*, Bloomington Ind.: Indiana University Press; revised edn., 1972.

Laurence, Margaret: *Long Drums and Cannons*, London: Macmillan, 1968.

Laye, Camara: *The African Child*, transl. James Kirkup, London: Fontana, 1959.

Lindfors, Bernth: 'The Palm Oil with which Achebe's words are eaten', *African Literature Today*, No. 1, 1968.

'Achebe on commitment and African writers', *Africa Report,* March 1970.

'The Blind Men and the Elephant', *African Literature Today,* No. 7, 1975.

(ed.) *Critical Perspectives on Nigerian Literatures,* London: Heinemann, 1979.

Lloyd, Peter C.: *Africa in Social Change,* London: Penguin Books, 1967.

Lukács, George: *The Meaning of Contemporary Realism,* transl. John and Necke Mander, London: Merlin Press, 1963.

Mazrui, Ali A.: *The Trial of Christopher Okigbo,* London: Heinemann, 1971.

*Political Values and the Educated Class in Africa,* London: Heinemann, 1978.

Mboya, Tom: *The Challenge of Nationhood,* London: Heinemann, 1970.

Miners, N.J.: *The Nigerian Army 1956-1966,* London: Methuen, 1971.

Moore, Gerald: *Wole Soyinka,* London: Evans Brothers, 1971.

Mphahlele, Ezekiel: *The African Image,* London: Faber and Faber; revised edn., 1974.

Ngugi wa Thiong'o: *A Grain of Wheat,* London: Heinemann, 1967.

*Homecoming,* London: Heinemann, 1967.

*Petals of Blood,* London, Heinemann, 1977.

Nigeria: Government White Paper: 'National Policy in Education', Lagos: Federal Ministry of Information, 1977.

Nkrumah, Kwame: *I Speak of Freedom,* London: Panaf Books, 1973.

Nyerere, Julius: *Ujamaa: Essays on Socialism,* Dar es Salaam: Oxford University Press, 1968.

Obiechina, Emmanuel: *Culture, Tradition and Society in the West African Novel,* Cambridge: Cambridge University Press, 1975.

O'Flinn, J.P.: 'Towards a Sociology of the Nigerian Novel', *African Literature Today,* No. 7, 1975.

Palmer, Eustace: *An Introduction to the African Novel,* London: Heinemann, 1972.

Peil, Margaret: *Nigerian Politics: The People's View,* London: Cassell, 1976.

Roscoe, Adrian A.: *Mother is Gold,* Cambridge: Cambridge University Press, 1971.

Sembène Ousmane: *God's Bits of Wood,* transl. Francis Price, London: Heinemann, 1970; reset 1976.

*Xala,* transl. Clive Wake, London: Heinemann, 1976.

Senghor, Léopold Sédar: *Prose and Poetry,* ed. and transl. John Reed and Clive Wake, London: Oxford University Press, 1965.

189

*Nocturnes*, transl. John Reed and Clive Wake, London: Heinemann, 1969.

Spencer, John (ed.): *The English Language in West Africa*, London: Longman, 1971.

Tighe, C.: 'In Detentio Preventione in Aeternum: Soyinka's *A Shuttle in the Crypt*', *Journal of Commonwealth Literature*, Vol. X, No. 3.

Walsh, William: *Commonwealth Literature*, London: Oxford University Press, 1973.

Wauthier, Claude: *The Literature and Thought of Modern Africa*, transl. Shirley Kay, London: Pall Mall Press, 1966.

Wilkinson, Nick: 'Demoke's Choice in Soyinka's *A Dance of the Forests*', *Journal of Commonwealth Literature*, Vol. X, No. 3.

Zell, Hans and Silver, Helene: *A Reader's Guide to African Literature*, London: Heinemann, 1972.

# INDEX